D1562249

A CLASSIC RETELLING

A Tale
OF TWO CITIES

by Charles Dickens

nextext

Picture Acknowledgements

Page 20: Copyright © Mary Evans Picture Library.

Table of Contents

The year is 1775. In England and France, there is struggle and bloodshed. Both countries are controlled by the rich, while almost everyone else is nearly starving.

In England, late one November night, Mr. Jarvis Lorry of Tellson's Bank travels by mail coach on a mysterious journey. His coach is stopped by a messenger, who gives him a note that reads, "Wait at Dover for Mam'selle."

Vocabulary words appear in boldface type and are
footnoted. Specialized or technical words and phrases
appear in lightface type and are footnoted.

Background

The French Revolution

The French Revolution (1789–1799) is one of the bloodiest and most violent events in world history. It is also one of the most important because it introduced the world to a new and powerful class of people: the middle class.

Historians still debate the causes of the French Revolution. Many blame the poor crop harvest of 1788. When the crops failed, people had no money to pay their taxes. They had no money for food. People in the cities and in the country began starving. All over France, poor working men, women, and children—called *peasants*—were turned out of their homes and forced to live in the streets and fields.

The French Aristocracy

In 1788, the French aristocracy was the ruling class of France. The aristocracy set the tax rates, owned most of the land, and employed the peasants as servants. (In *A Tale of Two Cities,* the Marquis St. Evrémonde is a member of this aristocracy, as is his nephew Charles Darnay.)

Because they were so poor and hungry, the peasants became resentful. Eventually, their resentment turned to anger and rage. Their rage was directed at what they believed was the source of their problems: the French aristocracy.

The Bastille

On July 14, 1789, a group of peasants stormed the Bastille, a huge prison on the outskirts of Paris. The crowd demanded that the guards give up the guns and ammunition stored there. When the guards refused, the crowd forced its way in and took command of the fortress.

Suddenly, there were riots all over France. Peasants robbed and burned the aristocrats' estates and threw their owners in prison. They imprisoned every aristocrat they could find, including King Louis XVI and his queen, Marie Antoinette.

The Reign of Terror

In the years following the storming of the Bastille, many aristocrats were put to death. Most were executed by guillotine, which became a symbol of the French Revolution. In 1799, a new constitution was drawn up, with Napoleon Bonaparte named as First Consul. Napoleon reorganized France. He declared that France would be governed by the *bourgeoisie*, or middle class. The French, he said, would never again feel the hunger that marked the year 1788.

Setting

Most of Dickens's novels are set in nineteenth-century Victorian England. In *A Tale of Two Cities*, however, the action occurs during the last part of the eighteenth century, from 1775 to approximately 1790. This was the period of the French Revolution, which began in 1789.

The action in *A Tale of Two Cities* takes place in two different cities: London and Paris. In Books One and Two, the action switches back and forth between the two cities. A small, poor village in a hollow in the French countryside also plays a part. In Book Three, the action occurs in Paris only.

In Paris, two places are of importance to the story: the Defarge wine shop and the prison called La Force, where Charles Darnay is imprisoned for treason. In London, the action centers around the Manette home in Soho and the main office of Tellson's Bank, which is where Mr. Lorry and Jerry Cruncher work.

Prison Gate This engraving of the Bastille entrance shows where a crowd confronted the guards to start the French Revolution.

Major Characters

In *A Tale of Two Cities*, some characters belong in the London group, some belong in Paris, and some belong in both places.

Sydney Carton

London Connection
born and raised in London but knows Paris well

Character Information
Carton is a kind-hearted, clever man who feels he has wasted his life. He drinks heavily and pays no attention to the damage he is doing to himself. He feels powerless to help himself or to change his ways.

Charles Darnay

London Connection
moves to London as a young man

Paris Connection
born outside of Paris to the noble St. Evrémond family

Character Information
As a child, Darnay was taught to hate the system by which a small number of aristocrats live off the sweat of hundreds of hungry peasants. He continues to fight this type of injustice as he grows into manhood.

Lucie Manette

London Connection
raised in London

Paris Connection
born in a small town outside of Paris

Character Information
Lucie is a beautiful, kind, and intelligent woman who is protective of her father, husband, and children. She feels deep loyalty to her friends and family and earns their loyalty in return.

Dr. Alexandre Manette

London Connection
lives in Soho with Lucie and Miss Pross

Paris Connection
born near Paris; imprisoned in the Bastille for 18 years

Character Information
Dr. Manette, father of Lucie, was imprisoned for all of Lucie's childhood. Although he is set free, Manette remains haunted by his years at the Bastille.

◀ Charles Darnay

Mr. Jarvis Lorry

London Connection
born and raised in London

Character Information
Mr. Lorry of Tellson's Bank feels at home in both Paris and London. He is, he insists, a "man of business." He is uncomfortable with displays of emotion.

Miss Pross

London Connection
born and raised in London

Character Information
Miss Pross is the Manettes' housekeeper and companion. She is loyal, loving, strong, and efficient.

Jerry Cruncher

London Connection
born and raised in London

Character Information
Cruncher is a messenger for Tellson's Bank by day. By night, he digs up bodies from graveyards and sells them to doctors for research.

Thérèse Defarge

Paris Connection
born outside of Paris; runs a wine shop in the heart of the city

Character Information
Madame Defarge is an angry revolutionary who wants to see the rich punished.

Ernest Defarge

Paris Connection
born outside of Paris; runs a wine shop in the heart of the city

Character Information
Ernest Defarge is not quite as angry as his wife, although he, too, is a revolutionary patriot. Even so, he feels a sense of loyalty to Dr. Manette, who was his master many years previously.

◀ Madame Thérèse Defarge

The Marquis St. Evrémonde ▶

Marquis St. Evrémonde

Paris Connection
born and raised outside of Paris

Character Information
The Marquis St. Evrémonde, also known as the Monseigneur or Monsieur the Marquis, lives on an estate outside of Paris. He believes very strongly that the old way—with peasants slaving for aristocrats—should continue. His nephew, Charles Darnay, disagrees.

Mr. Stryver

London Connection
born and raised in London

Character Information
Mr. Stryver, a successful lawyer, is Sydney Carton's boss. Stryver is proud and self-centered.

Historical Fiction

Made-up Characters and Real-life Events

A Tale of Two Cities is historical fiction. Dickens chose to use characters that he created to tell about true, important events. We care about the characters—Lucie Manette, her husband Charles Darnay, and their friend Sydney Carton. They get caught up in the passions of the French Revolution. In reading their story, we discover how dreadful some members of the aristocracy could be. We also discover how dreadful was the people's revenge.

The Marquis St. Evrémonde stands for the aristocracy. The vile things he and his family have done rouse the villagers and the working people in Paris to a frenzy. Charles Darnay, Lucie's husband, is a victim of their hatred because he is the nephew of the Marquis.

Lucie Manette, the sweet daughter of a kind and highly respected doctor, a young woman who has never hurt anyone, is threatened by the revolution because she married into the Evrémonde family.

A Mystery Story

Dickens chose to tell this story as a mystery story. He provided a character with a mysterious past—Dr. Manette. He leaves clues throughout the story—the ashes of a prisoner's writing found in a dungeon in a London prison, a tall stranger who hides under the Marquis's coach, a secret plan, and mysterious powders. The minor characters are very strange—spies, a grave digger, a woman called The Vengeance. These elements bring excitement and suspense to history.

Charles Dickens (1812–1870)

Born in 1812 to a large family, Dickens spent his early years in an English port town called Chatham. When he was twelve, he moved with his family to the city of London. He took a job in a factory after his father was thrown in jail for having debts. Later, he returned to school and worked as an errand-boy for a lawyer.

Dickens began to write for magazines when he was twenty-one and soon became a great success. Each week, readers waited eagerly for the next chapter to appear. With the publication of *The Pickwick Papers* in 1837, he became a celebrity. He wrote his popular historical novel *A Tale of Two Cities* in 1859.

▲

Charles Dickens

Charles Dickens

1812—Charles Dickens is born.

1823—His family moves to London. His father is imprisoned for debt. Dickens begins work in a factory.

1832—Charles Dickens begins publishing his writing in magazines.

1837—He becomes famous overnight with *The Pickwick Papers*.

1843—*A Christmas Carol* is published and becomes an instant success.

1859—*A Tale of Two Cities* is published.

1860–1861—*Great Expectations*, his greatest book, is published.

1870—Dickens dies suddenly, shortly after returning from a trip.

A CLASSIC RETELLING

Recalled to Life

Two Countries

It was the best of times, it was the worst of times, it was the age of wisdom, it was the age of foolishness; it was a time of belief, it was a time of **incredulity**,[1] it was the season of light, it was the season of darkness, it was the spring of hope, it was the winter of despair.[2] We had everything before us, we had nothing before us, we were all going direct to heaven, we were all going direct the other way.

It was the year of Our Lord, 1775. There was a king with a large jaw and a queen with a plain face on the throne of England; there was a king with

---

[1] **incredulity**—disbelief.

[2] These lines are famous, especially the first two phrases.

a large jaw and a queen with a fair face on the throne of France.[3] In both countries there was struggle and bloodshed, although worse was still to come. There were burglaries in open daylight and highway robberies in the dead of night. There were murders and kidnappings and attacks of all kinds. Poverty and despair were everywhere, and life for most people was nothing but struggle, struggle, struggle. Through it all, the hangman was kept busy stringing up rows of criminals, traitors, and innocents alike—all this in the name of protecting the **aristocracy**[4] and keeping the main streets and paths free of anything that was poor or shameful or ugly.

---

[3] King George III ruled England from 1760 to 1820. His wife was Charlotte Sophia of Mecklenburg-Strelitz. King Louis XVI ruled France from 1774 to 1792. His queen was Marie Antoinette.

[4] **aristocracy**—ruling class; the nobility.

The Road to Dover

We meet the first person of our story on the Dover[1] road. On this November night, the mist was thick and cold and clammy and the road was covered in thick mud. The mail-coach driver could hardly see the road ahead. Three passengers plodded beside the coach. The horses were tired, the driver had said, so the passengers would have to walk.

Although these three people walked together, each was very much alone. All three were hidden under many layers of coats and scarves, and each

---

[1] Dover—city in southeastern England. Travelers bound for France often cross the English Channel at Dover and arrive at the port of Calais, France.

set of eyes carefully avoided the others. In those days, travelers were shy of each other, for anybody on the road might be a robber or murderer.

An armed guard sat on a seat behind the driver. He kept his hand on the chest before him, where a loaded **blunderbuss**[2] lay on top of six or eight loaded horse-pistols, which lay atop a jumble of sharp knives and heavy wooden clubs.

"Tst, Joe!" cried the driver in a warning voice, looking down from his box.

"What do you hear, Tom?" They both listened.

"I hear a horse at a **canter**[3] coming up the hill, Joe. Gentlemen! In the king's name, all of you! Get aboard!" With this hurried order, he cocked his blunderbuss, and stood ready.

The passengers looked from the coachman to the guard, and from the guard to the coachman, and listened.

---

[2] **blunderbuss**—rifle.
[3] **canter**—an easy run between a trot and a gallop.

"So-ho!" the guard sang out, as loud as he could roar. "You there! Stop! I shall fire!"

The clop of hooves was suddenly quieter, and a man's voice called from the mist, "Is that the Dover mail? I have a message for one of your passengers."

"You there! Stop! I shall fire!"

"What passenger?"

"Mr. Jarvis Lorry."

One passenger showed in a moment that it was his name. The guard, the coachman, and the two other passengers eyed him distrustfully.

"What is the matter?" Mr. Lorry called out. "Who wants me? Is it Jerry?"

"I don't like Jerry's voice, if it is Jerry," growled the guard to himself. "He's hoarser than suits me, is Jerry."

"Yes, Mr. Lorry," Jerry answered.

"What is the matter?"

"A message sent after you from Tellson's."

"Come close, Jerry. The guard will allow it."

A horse and rider cut slowly through the mist and came to the side of the mail, where Mr. Lorry stood. The rider stooped and handed the passenger a small folded paper. "Guard!" said the passenger, in a tone of quiet confidence, "There is nothing to fear. I work for Tellson's Bank. You must know Tellson's Bank in London. I am going to Paris on business. Here's money for a drink. May I have a moment to read this message?"

"If you're quick, sir," the guard replied.

Mr. Lorry opened the envelope in the light of the coach-lamp, and read—first to himself and then aloud: "'Wait at Dover for Mam'selle.'"[4]

"It's not long, you see, guard," said Mr. Lorry thoughtfully. With this he turned to the messenger and said, "Jerry, say that my answer was, RECALLED TO LIFE."

Jerry jumped a little in his saddle. "That's a blazing strange answer," said he.

"Nevertheless, take that message back, and don't delay." With those words the passenger opened the coach-door and got in. After a moment, the coach moved on again.

---

[4] Mam'selle—an abbreviation of *Mademoiselle*, the French word for "Miss," or a young woman.

The Night Shadows

The mail coach moved slowly in the direction of Dover. Mr. Lorry sat in his seat with his eyes half closed. As he dozed, he saw before him the face of a man who had been buried alive.[1] It was a man of five-and-forty years. His face was badly wasted, but still—still! The dozing passenger could make out the pride and grief of his features. A hundred times Lorry asked of this **specter**:[2] "You've been buried how long?"

The answer was always the same: "Almost eighteen years."

---

[1] Dickens uses images of burial throughout the book.

[2] **specter**—ghost.

"You had abandoned all hope of being dug out?"

"Long ago," the ghost replied.

"You know that you are recalled to life?"

"They tell me so."

"Do you want to live?"

"I can't say," was the imagined response.

Mr. Lorry would then shake himself awake and lower the window to get the reality of mist and rain on his cheek. Yet, even when his eyes were opened on the mist and rain, the ghostly face would rise, and he would ask it again. "You have been buried how long?"

"Almost eighteen years."

"Do you want to live?"

"I can't say."

The weary passenger could still hear the words when he opened his eyes to daylight and found that the shadows of the night were gone. He lowered the window and looked out at the rising sun. "Eighteen years!" said the passenger aloud, looking at the sun. "Gracious Creator of day! To be buried alive for eighteen years!"

> *"You know that you are recalled to life?"*
>
> *"They tell me so."*

The Preparation

When the mail coach arrived in Dover, the porter at the Royal George Hotel opened the coach door. Mr. Lorry said impatiently, "Will there be a boat to Calais[1] tomorrow, porter?"

"Yes, sir, if the weather holds and the wind stays fair."

The porter showed Mr. Lorry to the coffee room. There he sat, a gentleman of sixty, formally dressed in a brown suit, which was well worn but very neat, with large square cuffs and large flaps on the pockets. Mr. Lorry's features were fine, although

---

[1] Calais—city in northern France on the Strait of Dover. Because it is just 21 miles from Dover, England, Calais is a major point for crossing the English Channel.

they, too, were a little worn. He wore an odd little **flaxen**[2] wig that looked as though it were spun from strands of silk or glass.

When his breakfast arrived, Mr. Lorry said to the porter, "I wish a room to be prepared for a young lady who may come here at any time today. She may ask for Mr. Jarvis Lorry, or she may only ask for a gentleman from Tellson's Bank. Please let me know."

"Yes, sir."

In a very few minutes, the waiter came in to announce that a Miss Manette had arrived from London and had asked to see the gentleman from Tellson's immediately.

M r. Lorry settled his odd little wig at his ears and followed the waiter to Miss Manette's room. It was a large, dark room, loaded with a heavy dark table. The two candles shed just a little light. The gloom of the room matched exactly the gloom in Mr. Lorry's heart.

By the light of the candles, Mr. Lorry saw a young lady of not more than seventeen, who was still holding her straw traveling hat by its ribbon in her

---

[2] **flaxen**—pale grayish yellow color; blonde. In those days, the upper-class men wore wigs.

hand. His eyes took in the short, pretty figure, a quantity of golden hair, and a pair of blue eyes that met his own with an inquiring look. He suddenly remembered a child he had held while crossing the English Channel on a cold day. Remembering his manners, he made a formal bow.

"Pray[3] take a seat, sir," said she in a very clear and pleasant young voice with just a trace of a foreign accent. "I received a letter from the Bank, sir, yesterday, informing me that some information about my poor father and his estate—"

Mr. Lorry moved in his chair, and cast a troubled look towards the back of the room.

"As I am an orphan with no one to protect me, I would consider it a great favor if the gentleman would escort me to France."

"—made it necessary that I should go to Paris and communicate with a gentleman of Tellson's Bank, who had been sent to Paris for that purpose."

"Myself."

"Yes. I replied to the Bank, sir, that as I am an orphan with no one to protect me, I would consider it a great favor if the gentleman would escort me to France."

---

[3] pray—please.

"I was happy," said Mr. Lorry, "to be given the charge."

"Sir, I thank you indeed. I thank you very gratefully. I am ready, now, to hear the nature of this business about my father."

After a pause, he said, with great **reluctance**,[4] "It is very difficult to begin."

The young woman looked thoughtful. "Are you a stranger to me, sir?" she asked.

Mr. Lorry opened his hands and shrugged. "Miss Manette, I am a man of business. It is my duty as a businessman to tell you a story. Think of me as a speaking machine, because truly, I am not much else. I will explain to you, miss, the story of one of our customers. This man, this customer—he was a French gentleman; a scientific gentleman; a man of great learning; a doctor."

"Was he from Beauvais?"[5]

"Why, yes, he was from Beauvais. Like Monsieur Manette, your father. And, like Monsieur Manette, your father, the gentleman had a fine reputation in Paris. I had the honor of knowing him there. Our relations were business relations, but confidential."

"When was this, sir?"

---

[4] **reluctance**—unwillingness.

[5] Beauvais—a town in France.

"I speak, miss, of twenty years ago. He married—an English lady—and I was one of the **trustees**.[6] Tellson's was his bank—"

"But this is my father's story, sir!" the young lady interrupted. "I begin to think that when my mother died—just two short years after my father died—it was you who brought me to England. This is why you look so familiar!"

Mr. Lorry took her hand and kissed it gently. "Miss Manette, it was I. You have been the **ward**[7] of Tellson's House ever since your mother died."

He continued. "So far, miss (as you have said), this is the story of your father. Now comes the difference. If your father had not died when he did—Don't be frightened! How you jump!"

She did, indeed, jump. And she caught his wrist with both her hands.

"Pray," said Mr. Lorry, in a soothing tone, bringing his left hand from the back of the chair to lay it on the trembling small fingers that clasped his sleeve, "pray control your trembling. This is a matter of business."

---

[6] **trustees**—those who hold legal title to property in order to administer it for a beneficiary.

[7] **ward**—minor who is placed under the care or protection of a guardian or court.

"As I was saying; if Monsieur Manette had not died—if he had been lost, or kidnapped, or kept in some godforsaken prison cell—then ... then the history of your father would have been the history of this unfortunate gentleman, the Doctor of Beauvais. Now if this doctor's wife, who was very brave, had suffered so much from her husband's disappearance before her little child was born—"

"The little child was a daughter, sir?"

"Yes—a daughter. Miss, if the poor lady had suffered so much before her little child was born that she came to the decision to spare the poor child any part of the agony of not knowing.... If she had allowed the little daughter to believe that her father was dead, and mentioned nothing of the disappearance—No, don't kneel! In heaven's name, why should you kneel to me?"

"Please, sir! I beg you for the truth!"

"Please! Be calm. This is business. Miss Manette, your mother took this course with you. And when she died, she left you, at two years old, to grow to be a blooming, beautiful, and happy young lady who knew nothing about her father's mysterious disappearance."

As he said these words he looked down, with pity, on the flowing golden hair. "You know that your father was not rich and that what he had was given to your mother and you. There has been no new discovery of money or property; but—"

He felt his wrist held closer, and he stopped. The expression in her eyes had deepened into one of pain and horror.

"—But he has been found. Your father is alive. He is greatly changed, probably, though we will hope for the best. Still, he is alive. He has been taken to the house of an old servant in Paris, and we are going there: I, to identify him, if I can; you, to restore him to life, love, duty, rest, and comfort."

> **"But he has been found. Your father is alive."**

A shiver ran through her frame. She said, in a low, distinct, **awe-stricken**[8] voice, "My father is alive."

"Only one thing more," said Mr. Lorry slowly. "It would be dangerous for us to ask questions about Dr. Manette. We must identify him and then return to England with him at once. If we must speak of the matter, we'll use my code phrase— 'Recalled to Life.' Above all else, we must be very, very careful. You and I and those like us have more enemies in France than you could ever meet in a lifetime."

---

[8] **awe-stricken**—full of wonder.

At the Wine Shop

Near a wine shop in the **wretched**[1] Saint Antoine district of Paris, a **cask**[2] of wine had fallen from a wagon into the street. The cask lay on its side, shattered like a walnut-shell. All the people within reach had stopped their business to run to the spot and drink the wine. The rough, uneven stones of the street had dammed the wine into little pools. Each little pool was surrounded by its own pushing and shoving crowd. Men and women kneeled down, made scoops of their two joined hands, and sipped. Others dipped in the puddles

[1] **wretched**—miserable.
[2] **cask**—keg.

with little mugs or even with handkerchiefs from women's heads, which were squeezed dry into infants' mouths. Others ran here and there, to cut off little streams of wine that started away in new directions.

In time, a different kind of blood would be spilled on the streets of this district. This was unavoidable in a place such as Saint Antoine, where the cold, dirt, sickness, ignorance, and want were ever present. People old and young shivered at every corner and suffered in every doorway. The children had ancient faces and grave voices, as did the mothers and fathers, the men and women. On every face, and heavy upon every brow, was the sign of hunger. Hunger was everywhere. It could be seen in the tall houses, in the torn clothes that hung upon the clotheslines, and in the straw and rags and wood that furnished every home. Hunger stared down from the smokeless chimneys and stared up from the filthy street. Hunger was written on the baker's shelves and on every dead-dog sausage that was offered for sale. Hunger rattled its dry bones among the roasting chestnuts in the fire; hunger was shred into atoms in every chip of potato fried in a few drops of oil.

In Saint Antoine, the streets were full of filth and **stench**.[3] And yet, in the eyes of the people, there was a fire—an anger—that could not be put out. With each hunger pang, the need to survive grew stronger. Men gathered in the stores and on the streets to make plans. They sharpened their knives and axes and kept

With each hunger pang, the need to survive grew stronger.

their guns oiled. The people of Saint Antoine knew that soon the time would come when they would make themselves heard. The time would come to tell the world about the darkness of their condition.

On the day the wine was spilled, the master of the wine shop stood outside and watched the struggle for the lost wine. "It's not my affair," said he, with a final shrug of his shoulders. "The people from the market broke the cask. Let them bring another."

This wine shop keeper—Monsieur Ernest Defarge—was a large man of thirty. On this bitterly cold day, he wore no coat, but carried one slung over his shoulder. His shirt-sleeves were rolled up, too, and his brown arms were bare to the elbows. He wore nothing on his head except his own

---

[3] **stench**—strong, foul odor; stink.

crisply curling short dark hair. He was clearly a man with a purpose—a man who would not change an opinion once that opinion had been voiced.

Madame Defarge, his wife, sat in the shop behind the counter as he came back inside. Madame Defarge was a large woman of about his own age, with a watchful eye, a steady face, and strong features, and a great calmness of manner. She laid down her knitting to pick her teeth with a toothpick. When Defarge came into the shop, she said nothing, but coughed just one small cough. This, in combination with the lifting of her dark eyebrows, suggested to her husband that he should look around the shop for the new customers who had dropped in while he was outside.

The wine shop keeper rolled his eyes about until they rested upon an elderly gentleman and a young lady who were seated in a corner. As he passed behind the counter, he noticed that the elderly gentleman said to the young lady, "This is our man."

He pretended not to notice the two strangers, and began talking with three customers who were drinking at the counter.

"How goes it, Jacques?"[4] said one of these three to Monsieur Defarge. "Is all the spilt wine swallowed?"

"Every drop, Jacques," answered Monsieur Defarge.

"It is not often," said the second of the three, addressing Monsieur Defarge, "that these miserable people know the taste of wine, or of anything but black bread and death. Is it not so, Jacques?"

"It is so, Jacques," Monsieur Defarge returned.

The last of the three said, "Ah! So much the worse! A bitter taste that these poor cattle always have in their mouths. Hard lives they live, Jacques. Am I right, Jacques?"

"You are right, Jacques," was the response of Monsieur Defarge. This third use of the name "Jacques" was finished at the moment when Madame Defarge put her toothpick aside. She took up her knitting and became absorbed in it.

"Gentlemen," said her husband, who had kept his bright eye observantly upon his wife, "The room that you wish to see is on the fifth floor. Since one of you has already been there, he can show the way. Gentlemen, **adieu!**"[5]

---

[4] The Defarges and others use the name "Jacques" as a code name for people who support the idea of a peasant revolt.

[5] **adieu**—good-bye.

They paid for their wine and left the place. The eyes of Monsieur Defarge were studying his wife at her knitting when the elderly gentleman approached the counter and asked to have a word with Defarge.

"Of course, sir," said Monsieur Defarge, and quietly stepped with him to the door. Their conference was very short, but very significant. They spoke for a minute and then Monsieur Defarge nodded and went out. The gentleman then **beckoned**[6] to the young lady, and they, too, went out. Madame Defarge knitted with nimble fingers and steady eyebrows, and saw nothing.

---

[6] **beckoned**—motioned her to come.

To the Garret

Mr. Jarvis Lorry and Miss Manette came out from the wine shop and joined Monsieur Defarge in the doorway, which opened into a stinking little black courtyard. From there they entered a gloomy tile-paved entry and stood at the bottom of a gloomy tile-paved staircase. Monsieur Defarge knelt down and put Miss Manette's hand to his lips. It was a gentle action, but not at all gently done. A remarkable change had come over Monsieur Defarge. He had no good humor left in his face. He had become a secret, angry, dangerous man.

"The stairs are very steep. Better to begin slowly." This, Monsieur Defarge, in a stern voice, said to Mr. Lorry, as they began climbing the filthy stairs.

"Is he alone?" Mr. Lorry whispered.

"Alone! Of course," said the other, in the same low voice.

"Is he always alone, then?"

"Yes."

At last they reached the top of the smelly main stairs. There was still an even steeper upper staircase to be climbed before the **garret**[1] story was reached. The keeper of the wine shop, always going a little in advance, took out a key.

"The door is locked then, my friend?" said Mr. Lorry, surprised.

"Ay. Yes," was the grim reply of Monsieur Defarge.

"You think it necessary to keep the poor man confined?"

"I think it necessary to turn the key. He has lived so long locked up that he would be frightened—go mad—tear himself to pieces, even—if his door was left open."

"Is it possible?" exclaimed Mr. Lorry.

"Is it possible?" repeated Defarge, bitterly. "Yes. In this world, anything that is ugly or unhappy or evil is possible."

---

[1] **garret**—attic.

They went up slowly and softly. The staircase was short, and they were soon at the top. There they came upon three men, whose heads were bent down close together, and who were looking through some holes in the door. On hearing footsteps, these three turned, and rose, and showed themselves to be the three men named Jacques who had been drinking in the wine shop.

"I forgot them in the surprise of your visit," explained Monsieur Defarge. "Leave us, good boys; we have business here."

The three passed by and went silently down. The wine shop keeper went straight to the door that the men had been peeking through. Mr. Lorry asked him in a whisper, with some anger: "Do you make a show of Monsieur Manette?"

"I show him, in the way you have seen, to a chosen few."

"Who are the few? How do you choose them?"

"I choose men of my own name—Jacques is my name—to whom the sight is likely to do good."

With this, he knocked loudly on the door and then turned his key. The door slowly opened inward under his hand, and he looked into the room and said something. A faint voice answered.

He looked back over his shoulder and beckoned them to enter. Mr. Lorry got his arm securely round Miss Manette's waist and held her; for he felt that she was sinking.

"It's—it's business, business!" he urged, with a moisture that was not of business shining on his cheek. "Come in, come in!" Because he was desperate, he lifted her a little, and hurried her into the room.

Defarge closed the door and locked it from the inside, walked slowly across the room, stopped, and turned around. The garret, built to be a storage room for firewood and the like, was dim and dark. It was difficult, on first coming in, to see anything. After a moment, however, their eyes adjusted and were drawn to the one small window, where a white-haired man, whose back was toward the door, sat on a low bench, busily making shoes.

BOOK ONE

The Shoemaker

"Good day!" said Monsieur Defarge, looking down
at the white head that bent low over the shoemaking.

A very faint voice responded to the greeting, as
if it were at a distance: "Good day!"

"You are still hard at work, I see?"

After a long silence, the head was lifted for
another moment, and the voice replied, "Yes—I
am working." This time, a pair of **haggard**[1] eyes
looked quickly at the questioner, before the face
dropped again.

The faintness of the man's voice was pitiful and
dreadful. It was not the faintness of physical

---

[1] **haggard**—worn out, wild looking.

weakness, but of solitude and lack of use. It was like the last feeble echo of a sound made long ago.

"I want," said Defarge, who had not moved his gaze from the shoemaker, "to let in a little more light here. Can you bear a little more?"

The shoemaker stopped his work and looked up. "What did you say?"

"Can you bear a little more light?"

"I *must* bear it, if you let it in."

Defarge opened the shutters on the window a bit more. A broad ray of light fell into the garret, and showed the workman with an unfinished shoe upon his lap. His few tools and various scraps of leather were at his feet and on his bench. He had a white beard, raggedly cut, but not very long, a hollow face, and very bright eyes. His yellow rags of shirt lay open at the throat, and showed his body to be withered and worn.

"Are you going to finish that pair of shoes today?" asked Defarge, motioning to Mr. Lorry to come forward.

"I suppose so. I don't know."

Mr. Lorry came silently forward, leaving the daughter by the door. When he had stood, for a minute or two, by the side of Defarge, the shoemaker looked up. He showed no surprise at seeing another figure.

"What is your name?" Mr. Lorry asked in a gentle voice.

"What did you say? Did you ask me for my name?"

"Yes, I did."

"One Hundred and Five, North Tower."

"Is that your name?"

"One Hundred and Five, North Tower."

With a weary sound that was not a sigh, nor a groan, the shoemaker bent to work again.

Defarge said to Mr. Lorry in a low voice, "One Hundred and Five, North Tower was his prison cell. If you ask a question of him that he cannot answer, he will simply repeat this phrase."

Mr. Lorry said to the bent figure: "Monsieur Manette, do you remember nothing of me?"

The shoe dropped to the ground, and he sat looking fixedly at the questioner.

"Monsieur Manette," Mr. Lorry said as he laid his hand upon Defarge's arm. "Do you remember nothing of this man? Look at him. Look at me. Do you see your old banker and your old servant?"

The prisoner of many years sat looking fixedly, by turns, at Mr. Lorry and at Defarge. There seemed to be no light of recognition in his eyes.

After a deep, long sigh, he took the shoe up and resumed his work.

Slowly, the young lady moved from the wall of the garret to very near the bench on which the shoemaker sat. Not a word was spoken, not a sound was made. She stood, like a spirit, beside him, and he bent over his work.

Eventually, his eyes caught sight of the skirt of her dress. He looked up, and saw her face. The shoemaker stared at her with a fearful look, and after a while his lips began to form some words, though no sound proceeded from them. After a moment, he said quietly, "What is this?"

With tears streaming down her face, she put her two hands to her lips, and kissed them to him; then clasped them on her breast, as if she laid his ruined head there.

"You are not the **gaoler's**[2] daughter?"

She sighed, "No."

"Who are you?"

Not yet trusting her voice, she sat down on the bench beside him. He **recoiled**,[3] but she laid her

---

[2] **gaoler's**—jail-keeper's. The word *gaol* is the British word for *jail*.

[3] **recoiled**—jumped back, as in fear or disgust.

hand upon his arm. A strange thrill struck him when she did so; he laid the knife down softly, and sat staring at her.

Her golden hair, which she wore in long curls, had been hurriedly pushed aside and fell down over her neck. Advancing his hand by little and little, he took it up and looked at it. Next he put his hand to his neck, and took off a blackened string with a scrap of folded rag attached to it. He opened this, carefully, on his knee. The scrap contained one or two long golden hairs.

He took her hair into his hand again, and looked closely at it. "It is the same. How can it be? How can it be?" He turned her full to the light, and looked at her and said slowly, "She laid her head upon my shoulder that night when I was **summoned out**[4]—she had a fear of my going, though I had none—and when I was brought to the North Tower, they found these golden strands upon my sleeve. 'Will you let me keep them?' I asked. 'They can never help me to escape in the body, though they may in the spirit.' Those were the words I said. I remember them very well."

"Can it be you? No, no, no; you are too young, too blooming. It can't be. What is your name, my gentle angel?"

---

[4] **summoned out**—sent for.

Hearing his softer tone and manner, his daughter fell upon her knees before him, with her hands upon his breast, and said: "O, sir, I am your daughter! My dearest dear, your agony is over. I have come here to take you away. We will go to England to be at peace and at rest. My honored father, I beg your pardon for having never searched for you! If only I had known!

> *"O, sir, I am your daughter! My dearest dear, your agony is over. I have come here to take you away."*

"O, Mr. Lorry! I feel his tears upon my face, and his sobs strike against my heart. O, thank God, he understands!"

When all was quiet again, the young woman said, "If, without disturbing him, all could be arranged for us to leave Paris at once, so that, from this very door, he could be taken away—"

"But, consider. Is he fit for the journey?" asked Mr. Lorry.

"More fit for that, I think, than to remain in this city that has been so dreadful to him," she replied.

"It is true," said Defarge. "Monsieur Manette is, for all reasons, best out of France."

"Then be so kind," urged Miss Manette, "as to leave us here. I will take care of him until you return, and then we will leave straight away."

By the time night had fallen, Mr. Lorry and Monsieur Defarge had assembled what was needed for the journey. They had brought with them some traveling cloaks, bread, meat, wine, and hot coffee. The old man had a wild, lost manner, yet he took pleasure in the sound of his daughter's voice and always turned to it when she spoke. When she asked him to go down the stairs, he obeyed without complaint. Once on the street, he got into a coach and his daughter followed. At the last moment, he asked for his shoemaking tools and the unfinished shoes. Madame Defarge (who had been knitting nearby) said that she would get them, and hurried up the stairs. She quickly brought his tools down and handed them into the carriage.

Defarge called to the driver: "To Calais!" The **postilion**[5] cracked his whip, and the carriage clattered away.

THE END OF BOOK ONE

---

[5] **postilion**—one who rides near the lead horse to guide the team of horses pulling a coach.

The Golden Thread

Five Years Later

Tellson's Bank by Temple Bar[1] was an old-
fashioned place, even in the year 1780. It was very
small, very dark, very ugly, and very uncomfortable.
It was perfectly inconvenient, and the old partners
were proud of it. Outside Tellson's—never by any
means in it, unless called in—was an odd-job-man,
an occasional porter and messenger. He was never
absent during business hours, unless upon an
errand, and then he was represented by his son, a
filthy **urchin**[2] of twelve, who looked just like his
father. The man's name was Jerry Cruncher; the
son's name was Jerry as well.

---

[1] Temple Bar—a gate that marked the formal entrance to the City of London.
[2] **urchin**—playful or mischievous youngster; scamp.

One windy March morning in the year 1780, Jerry Cruncher was called into the Bank for an important errand.

"You know the Old Bailey[3] well, no doubt?" said one of the oldest bank clerks to Jerry.

"Ye-es, sir," returned Jerry. "I do know the Bailey."

"Very well. Find the door where the witnesses go in, and show the doorkeeper this note for Mr. Lorry. The doorkeeper will let you in and pass the note to Mr. Lorry. Then wait in the courtroom until Mr. Lorry wants you."

"Is that all, sir?"

"That's all. He wishes to have a messenger at hand. Here is the letter. Go along."

Jerry took the letter, tipped his hat, and went his way.

---

[3] Old Bailey—the main criminal court in London.

The Trial of Treason

Making his way through the crowd gathered at the front of the Old Bailey, the messenger found the door for witnesses and handed in his letter through a slot in it.

After some delay, the door slowly turned on its hinges and allowed Mr. Jerry Cruncher to squeeze himself into court.

"What's on?" he asked, in a whisper, of the man he found himself next to.

"The treason case."

Presently, the **dock**[1] became the central point of interest. Two gaolers, who had been standing there,

---

[1] **dock**—an enclosed place where the defendant stands or sits in a court of law.

went out, and the prisoner was brought in. Everybody stared, anxious for a glimpse of the man. The prisoner was a young man around twenty-five years old. He was well grown and well groomed and looked like a young gentleman.

Then the announcement: "Silence in the court! The prisoner, Charles Darnay, yesterday pleaded not guilty to the charge of treason. He is accused of assisting Louis, the French king,[2] in his wars against our excellent country."

The accused did not **flinch**[3] at the announcement. He was quiet and attentive, and he watched the proceedings with a serious interest. As he looked around the room, he caught sight of two persons who interested him enormously.

The first of the two was a young lady of little more than twenty. Next to her sat a gentleman who was clearly her father. He was memorable because of the whiteness of his hair and his thoughtful expression. On the daughter's face was both terror and pity. Her distress was so noticeable that the whisper went about, "Who are they?"

Jerry, the messenger, stretched his neck to hear who they were. "Witnesses," someone told him.

"For which side?" asked Jerry.

---

[2] the French king—Louis XVI of France.
[3] **flinch**—draw back or jerk away.

"Against the prisoner."

The Judge, whose eyes had gone in the direction of the young lady, turned back to the bar and looked steadily at the man whose life was in his hands as Mr. Attorney General[4] rose to spin the rope, grind the ax, and hammer the nails into the **scaffold**.[5]

M<small>r.</small> Attorney General told the jury that the prisoner before them, though young in years, was highly experienced in the practice of treason. Certain lists, not in his own handwriting, had been found in his desk by his servant. These lists, which contained information about the English army and navy, had been given to a foreign power. For several minutes he proceeded to describe how very patriotic and loyal his witnesses would be. As soon as he stopped speaking, the first of his witnesses, Mr. John Barsad, appeared in the witness box.

The Solicitor General,[6] a Mr. Stryver, who had been retained as an attorney for the accused, stood up and made a humble bow to the jury. After a

---

[4] Attorney General—the prosecutor.

[5] **scaffold**—platform used in the execution of condemned prisoners, as by hanging or beheading.

[6] Solicitor General—the defense lawyer.

brief speech in which he explained his background and qualifications, he introduced his most learned assistant, Mr. Carton, who bore a striking resemblance to the prisoner.[7] Mr. Carton, however, barely glanced up at the introduction, so busy was he with the papers in front of him.

Without further delay, Mr. Stryver announced that he had some questions for the witness. He turned to Mr. Barsad with a determined look on his face. Had Mr. Barsad ever been a spy himself? No, the witness replied **scornfully**.[8] Had he ever been in prison? Certainly not. Never in a debtors' prison?[9] Didn't see what that had to do with anything. Come, once again. Never? Yes. How many times? Two or three times. Not five or six? Perhaps. Ever borrow money from the prisoner? Yes. Ever repay him? No.

The questions seemed to go on forever, and yet the Solicitor General's point was made: this John Barsad, whom the Attorney General had called "**virtuous**,"[10] was a liar and a thief.

---

[7] Carton's physical appearance becomes increasingly important as the novel continues.

[8] **scornfully**—mockingly.

[9] debtors' prison—a jail reserved for those owing money or property.

[10] **virtuous**—having or showing virtue, especially moral excellence.

After Mr. Lorry testified that he had seen the accused come aboard ship in Calais, the next virtuous witness, Roger Cly, revealed himself to be just as dishonest. He too was picked apart by Mr. Stryver, as the Attorney General covered his eyes with his hands.

The next witness was a Miss Lucie Manette. "Miss Manette, look upon the prisoner. Have you seen him before?"

"Yes, sir."

"Where?"

"On board the packet-ship from Calais to Dover. We were on our way from Paris to London."

"Miss Manette, did you have any conversation with the prisoner on that trip across the Channel?"[11]

"Yes, sir."

"Repeat it for us, please."

"When the gentleman—the prisoner—came on board, he noticed that my father was very tired and weak. He said he would help me care for my father. That was when we began speaking."

"Let me interrupt you for a moment. Had he come on board alone?"

"No."

---

[11] Channel—the English Channel divides England and France.

"How many were with him?"

"Two French gentlemen."

"Did they speak together?"

"They spoke together until the French gentlemen had to get back on their boat."

"Were any papers passed back and forth between them, similar to these lists?"

"They did have some papers, but I don't know what they were. They were similar in size to what you hold."

"Now recall the prisoner's conversation, Miss Manette."

"He told me that he was traveling on secret business, which might get people into trouble, and that he was therefore traveling under an assumed name. He said that this business had, within a few days, taken him to France, and might take him backwards and forwards between France and England for a long time to come."

Mr. Attorney General then called some more witnesses who swore that they had often seen in the prisoner's possession papers with military information. The crowd in the courtroom looked at each other knowingly.

An unusual thing happened then. A witness was asked if he was sure that he had seen the prisoner only once. The prisoner's counsel asked if he was sure it was the same person. He was. "Did you ever see anyone who looked like the prisoner?" Not so like that he could be mistaken. "Look at my learned friend Mr. Carton, and then at the prisoner. Are they like each other?"

They were enough like each other to surprise everyone present.

After an hour and a half, the jury was back again—much to the surprise of everyone involved. They had made their decision.

"Acquitted" was the message Jerry carried back to the Bank from Mr. Lorry.

"If you had sent the message 'recalled to life' again," muttered Jerry as he left, "I should have known what you meant, this time."

After some delay, Dr. Manette, Lucie Manette, Mr. Lorry, and Mr. Stryver, who was Charles Darnay's attorney, emerged from the dim and grim corridors of the courtroom. They gathered round Mr. Charles Darnay—the former prisoner—and congratulated him on his escape from death. Mr. Darnay kissed Lucie's hand **fervently**[12] and gratefully and then turned to Mr. Stryver, whom he warmly thanked.

---

[12] **fervently**—with much feeling.

All the while, Dr. Manette stared at Mr. Darnay. On his face was a deep frown of dislike and mistrust, not unmixed with fear. Miss Manette, upon seeing her father's distress, took hold of his hand.

"My father," said Lucie, softly. "Shall we go home, my father?"

With a long breath, he answered "Yes. We'll go home now, my darling."

Hundreds of People

The **lodgings**[1] of Dr. Manette were on a quiet street corner not far from Soho[2] square. The Doctor occupied two floors of a large house. On the first level, he received patients who came because of his old reputation and scientific knowledge. He made his home on the second level. With him lived his dear daughter, Lucie, and their housekeeper, Miss Pross.

A short four months after Mr. Darnay's trial for treason, Mr. Jarvis Lorry walked along the sunny streets of Soho, on his way to dine with the Doctor.

---

[1] **lodgings**—living quarters.
[2] Soho—a London neighborhood.

Mr. Lorry had become the Doctor's friend, and the quiet street corner was a sunny part of his life.

Arriving at the door of Dr. Manette's house, Mr. Lorry looked about. No one was in sight. He rang the door bell and waited patiently. The maid showed him in and asked him to wait.

"How do you do?" inquired Miss Pross, a strong red-haired woman, as she entered the room.

"I am pretty well, I thank you," answered Mr. Lorry, a bit meekly, for he was intimidated by Miss Pross. "How are you?"

"Nothing to boast of," said Miss Pross.

"Indeed?"

"Ah! Indeed!" said Miss Pross. "I am very much put out about my Ladybird!"[3]

"Indeed?"

"For gracious sake, say something else besides 'indeed,' or you'll irritate me to death," said Miss Pross.

"Really, then?" said Mr. Lorry, cautiously.

"'Really' is bad enough," returned Miss Pross, "but better. Yes, I am very much put out."

"May I ask the cause?"

"I don't want dozens of people, who are not at all worthy of Ladybird, to come here calling on her," said Miss Pross.

---

[3] Ladybird—a term of affection that Miss Pross uses for Lucie Manette.

"Do dozens come for that purpose?"

"Hundreds," said Miss Pross.

"Dear me!" said Mr. Lorry, as the safest remark he could think of.

"I have lived with the darling since she was ten years old. And it's really very hard," said Miss Pross. "All sorts of people who are not in the least degree worthy of my sweet are always turning up," said Miss Pross.

Mr. Lorry knew Miss Pross to be very jealous, but also very loyal.

"There never was, nor will be, but one man worthy of Ladybird," said Miss Pross, "and that was my brother Solomon, if he hadn't made a mistake in life."

Miss Pross's brother Solomon was a heartless **scoundrel**[4] who had taken everything she owned, and had left her in her poverty forevermore, without ever looking back.

Rather than comment on Solomon, Mr. Lorry thought it wise to change the subject. "As we happen to be alone for the moment, and are both people of business," he said, "let me ask you—does

---

[4] **scoundrel**—wicked villain.

the Doctor, in talking with Lucie, ever refer to his imprisonment?"

"Never."

"And yet he keeps his shoemaker's bench and tools in his room?"

"Yes!" returned Miss Pross, shaking her head. "But I don't say he don't refer to it within himself."

"Do you suppose," Mr. Lorry went on, "that Dr. Manette has any theory of his own about why he was imprisoned for all those long years, or even about who was responsible?"

"I think he has a theory, though he's never shared it."

"Isn't it remarkable that Dr. Manette, who is innocent of any crime, should never touch upon that question?"

"Well! To the best of my understanding, he is afraid of the whole subject."

"Afraid?"

"It's plain enough, I should think, why he may be. It's a dreadful memory. Besides that, his loss of himself grew out of it. Not knowing how he lost himself, or how he recovered himself, he may never feel certain of not losing himself again. That alone would make the subject unpleasant, I should think."

With that deep remark, Miss Pross stood and motioned to Mr. Lorry. "Ah, here they are. Now we shall have hundreds of people pretty soon!"

Miss Pross took off her darling's bonnet and smoothed her rich hair. The Doctor, looking at them, told Miss Pross how she spoilt Lucie.

At dinner time, the hundreds of people still had not come. As it was a hot day, Lucie suggested that the wine should be carried out under the shade tree, and they should sit there in the air. Still, the hundreds of people did not present themselves. Mr. Darnay came to call while they were sitting under the tree, but he was the only one.

Dr. Manette received him kindly, and so did Lucie.

"Pray, Dr. Manette," said Mr. Darnay, as they sat under the tree, "have you seen much of the Tower?"[5]

"Lucie and I have been there; but only casually."

"I have been there, as you remember, in another character," said Darnay with a smile, though

---

[5] The Tower of London is a building complex at the edge of the City of London. The structure includes thirteen towers, the most infamous of which is the Bloody Tower. Many memorable people were imprisoned in the Tower, and some of them, including Lady Jane Grey, Thomas More, and Sir Walter Raleigh, were executed there.

reddening a little angrily. "They told me an interesting thing when I was there."

"In making some repairs, the workmen came upon an old **dungeon**,[6] which had been, for many years, built up and forgotten. Every stone of its inner wall was covered by prisoners' carvings—dates, names, complaints, and prayers. Upon a corner stone in an angle of the wall, one prisoner had cut three letters. They were done with some very poor instrument, and hurriedly, with an unsteady hand. At first, they were read as D. I. C.; but, on more careful examination, the last letter was found to be G. It was suggested that the letters were not initials, but the complete word, DIG. The floor beneath the inscription was very carefully examined, and ashes of a paper mingled with the ashes of a small leather case or bag were found. What the unknown prisoner had written will never be read, but he had written something, and hidden it away to keep it from the gaoler."

"My father," exclaimed Lucie, "you are ill!"

---

[6] **dungeon**—prison cell. The theme of well-known lost papers will be repeated later in the book.

Dr. Manette had suddenly started up, with his hand to his head. His manner and his look quite terrified them all.

"No, my dear, not ill. There are large drops of rain falling, and they made me start. We had better go in."

Later, at teatime, there were still no hundreds of people. Mr. Sydney Carton, a lawyer in Mr. Stryver's firm, lounged in, but he made only two.

The street resounded with the echoes of footsteps coming and going.

Lucie sat by her father at the window; Darnay sat beside her; and Carton leaned against a window. There was a great hurry in the streets as people sped away to get shelter before the storm broke. The street resounded with the echoes of footsteps coming and going, yet not one was in sight.

"Sometimes," Lucie began with a thoughtful air, "sometimes I have sat alone here on an evening, listening, until I believe I am hearing the echoes of all the footsteps that are coming by-and-by into our lives."

"There is a great crowd coming into our lives, if that be so," Sydney Carton struck in, in his moody way.

The footsteps were **incessant**,[7] and the hurry of them became more and more rapid. "Are all these footsteps destined to come to all of us, Miss Manette, or are we to divide them among us?" Mr. Darnay asked.

"I don't know, Mr. Darnay; it was a foolish fancy. And yet I imagine they are the footsteps of the people who are to come into my life, and my father's."

"There is a great crowd bearing down upon us, Miss Manette, and I see them—by the lightning," said Carton, after a vivid flash of lightning.

"And I hear them," he added again, after a peal of thunder. "Here they come, fast, fierce, and furious."

The little group listened to the footsteps in silence. The storm, which had been slow in coming, was now upon them. It rained and thundered until after the moon rose at midnight.

---

[7] **incessant**—never stopping. Watch for more references to the sound of footsteps.

BOOK TWO

Monseigneur in the City

Monsieur the Marquis,[1] one of the great lords in power at the Court,[2] held a **lavish**[3] reception at his grand hotel in Paris. Only the most important men and women in the Court were invited, and only the finest food and wine were served. All this was prepared in the back rooms of the grand hotel by the torn and ragged men and women who served the Monseigneur[4] for just pennies a day. Without a

---

[1] Marquis—a nobleman ranking below a duke and above an earl or a count.

[2] Court—the people who were closest in rank to the king and queen.

[3] **lavish**—extravagant.

[4] Monseigneur—a title given to an eminent French person. In *A Tale of Two Cities*, the title Monseigneur is used interchangeably with the title Monsieur the Marquis.

word of thanks or kindness, Monseigneur took their hard work and obedience for granted. Nothing less was expected, for he was (in his own mind) the finest man in all of Paris. The Marquis was a tall man of about sixty, handsomely dressed, with a face like a fine mask. His nose, beautifully formed, had two small dimples at the top of each nostril, and these were the only part of his face that ever changed.

After the reception had ended, Monseigneur called for his carriage and told the driver to make haste, make haste, make haste, as the drive ahead was long and tiresome. With a wild rattle and clatter, the carriage dashed through streets and swept round corners, with women screaming before it, and men clutching each other and clutching children out of its way. At last, swooping around a street corner by a fountain, one of its wheels came to a sickening little jolt, and there was a loud cry from a number of voices, and the horses reared and plunged. With that, the carriage came to an abrupt halt.

"What has gone wrong?" said Monsieur, calmly looking out.

A tall man in a nightcap had caught up a bundle from among the feet of the horses, and had laid it on the basement of the fountain, and was down in the mud and wet, howling over it like a wild animal.

"Pardon, Monsieur the Marquis!" said a ragged and submissive man. "It is a child."

"Why does he make that horrible noise? Is it his child?"

"Excuse me, Monsieur the Marquis—it is a pity—yes."

"Killed!" shrieked the man in wild desperation, extending both arms above his head, and staring at Monsieur the Marquis. "Dead!"

The people closed round, and stared at Monsieur the Marquis. There was no visible anger in the stares, and yet they continued to watch him in silence. Monsieur the Marquis ran his eyes over them all, as if they were rats that had come out of their holes. He took out his purse.

"It is extraordinary to me," said he, "that you people cannot take care of yourselves and your children. One or the other of you is forever in the way. How do I know what injury you have done my horses? Here! Give him that."

He threw out a gold coin for the valet to pick up, and the eyes of the crowd watched the coin as it fell.

The tall man called out again with a most unearthly cry, "Dead!"

He was cut off by the quick arrival of another man. On seeing him, the miserable

> **"It is better for the poor little plaything to die so than to live."**

creature fell upon his shoulder, sobbing and crying.

"I know all, I know all," said the man who had just arrived. "Be a brave man, my Gaspard! It is better for the poor little plaything to die so than to live. It has died in a moment without pain. Could it have lived an hour as happily?"

"You are a philosopher, you there," said the Marquis, smiling. "What is your name?"

"They call me Defarge."

"What is your trade?"

"Monsieur the Marquis, I am a vendor of wine."

"Pick up that, philosopher and vendor of wine," said the Marquis, throwing him another gold coin, "and spend it as you will.[5] The horses there; are they all right?"

---

[5] The Marquis gave the same amount of money to a father whose child had been killed and to someone who amused him. Dickens uses this to tell you what sort of man the Marquis was.

Without waiting for an answer, Monsieur the Marquis gave the order to drive away. He had the air of a gentleman who had accidentally broken some common thing, had paid for it, and could afford to pay for it. Suddenly, his ease was disturbed by a coin flying into his carriage.

"Hold!" said Monsieur the Marquis. "Hold the horses! Who threw that coin?"

He looked to the spot where Defarge the vendor of wine had stood a moment before; but the man was gone. In his place was the figure of a dark, stout woman, knitting.

"You dogs!" said the Marquis, but smoothly, "I would ride over any of you very willingly, and exterminate you from the earth. If I knew which rascal threw that at my carriage, he should be crushed under the wheels."

Again, no one said a word. But the woman who stood knitting looked steadily at the Marquis. Without noticing her, the Marquis said, "Go on!" and off they sped.

BOOK TWO

Monseigneur in the Country

Monsieur the Marquis sat in comfort as his coach rolled slowly up a steep hill. At the top, he looked down at a little village, a church tower, a windmill, a forest for hunting, and an old stone building that was used as a prison. The village in the hollow had its one poor street, with its poor brewery, poor **tannery**,[1] poor tavern, and a poor stableyard for a group of poor horses. All the people in the village were poor, and many of them went night after night without any supper at all.

The people of the village were poor mostly because of the Marquis and the aristocracy he

---

[1] **tannery**—place where leather is cured.

represented. They paid taxes to the state, taxes to the church, taxes to the lord, taxes to the local government, and taxes to the general government. It was a wonder that there was any village left unswallowed.

Monsieur the Marquis cast his eyes to the left, and looked with mistrust at a man who had been following the carriage for quite a distance. With an impatient gesture, he called out, "Bring me that fellow!"

The fellow was brought, cap in hand, to speak to the Monseigneur.

"I passed you on the road?"

"Monseigneur, it is true."

"Why were you staring so?"

"Monseigneur, I looked at the man." He stooped a little, and with his tattered blue cap pointed under the carriage.

"What man, pig?"

"Pardon, Monseigneur; he was there, hanging by the chain of your coach."

"May the Devil carry away these idiots! Who was the man? You know all the men of this part of the country. Who was he?"

"Your pardon, Monseigneur! He was not of this part of the country."

"He was swinging by the chain?"

"Yes, Monseigneur. His head hanging over—like this!"

"What was he like?"

"Monseigneur, he was whiter than the miller. All covered with dust, white as a specter, tall as a specter!"

"Truly, you did well," said the Marquis, "to see a thief under my carriage and not to have told me sooner! Bah! Move aside!"

The carriage continued on its way. The sweet scents of the summer night rose all around him, although the Monseigneur took no notice. At last he was at the front door of his château.[2] Without so much as a glance at the porter, Monseigneur growled, "Monsieur Charles, whom I expect: is he arrived from England?"

"Monseigneur, he is here, in your drawing room."[3]

U_p the broad flight of shallow steps marched Monsieur the Marquis. The great door clanged behind him, and he crossed a great hall that

---

[2] château—a French manor house.

[3] drawing room—a room used to receive visitors who came to pay formal calls during the afternoon. It was also used as a room for the ladies to assemble after dinner.

was grim with old boarspears, swords, and hunting knives.

He passed into a large room and stood staring at his nephew Charles, who was known in England as Charles Darnay. Monseigneur greeted him in a polite manner, but they did not shake hands.

"You have been a long time coming," said the Marquis, with a smile.

"On the contrary, I came direct."

"Pardon me! I meant not a long time on the journey; a long time including the journey."

"I have come back, sir, as you anticipate, pursuing the object that took me away. It has carried me unto great and unexpected danger; but it is a sacred object, and if it had carried me to death I hope it would have sustained me."

"It is not necessary to say to death," said the uncle.

"For anything I know," the nephew went on, "you may have worked to make me more suspicious. I know you would stop me by any means—even send me to prison."

"It is possible," said the uncle calmly. "I could even inconvenience you to that extent."

After a pause, Charles said. "I have come back, sir, to discuss my **station**[4] as your nephew and sole heir."

"Ah, yes. Your station and name."

"I will tell you now that I believe our family name—the name of Evrémonde—is the most hated in all of France."

"Let us hope so," said the uncle. "It is the job of the low people to dislike those of our station."

> *"I will tell you now that I believe our family name—the name of Evrémonde—is the most hated in all of France."*

"There is not," continued the nephew, "a face I can look at, in all this country round about us, that looks at me with any kindness."

"A compliment," said the Marquis, "to the grandeur of our family. Hah! **Repression**[5] is the only thing that works with these people," he continued. "So long as they fear and despise you, they will remain your slaves."

"Sir," said the nephew, "we have done wrong and are reaping the fruits of wrong."

---

[4] **station**—social position; rank.
[5] **Repression**—keeping down by force, holding back natural development.

"We have done wrong?" repeated the Marquis, with a small smile.

"We have injured every human creature who has come between us and our pleasure, whatever it was. And now I am responsible for a system that I despise. I want to help these people, but I cannot because of my rank." With a small shake of his head, Charles continued sadly: "This property and all of France are lost to me. I **renounce**[6] them. You may keep it all. There is a curse on it, and on all this land."

"Hah!" said the Marquis again, in a well-satisfied manner. "And you? Forgive my curiosity; how do you, under your new philosophy, intend to support yourself?"

"I must do what others of our station may have to do sometime—I will work. I will leave here and go to England."

"Well," said the Marquis. "It's all settled. Now, as I am tired, I will go to bed."

---

[6] **renounce**—to give up (a title, for example), especially by formal announcement.

Early the next morning, a **valet**[7] came to wake the Marquis. Cautiously, he pulled back the bed-curtains, expecting an angry outburst from within. Instead, however, the eyes of the valet fell upon what appeared to be a fine stone mask, frozen in a position of anger and fear. Driven home into the heart of the stone figure was a knife. Around its blade was a bit of paper, on which was scrawled: "Drive him fast to his tomb. This, from JACQUES."

Monsieur the Marquis had been murdered in the night.

---

[7] **valet**—a man's male servant, who takes care of his clothes and performs other personal services.

BOOK TWO

Two Promises

Twelve months had come and gone, and Mr.
Charles Darnay was working in England as a
French tutor and translator. Even with a new job
and a new station, Darnay still found time to think
about the one who had been in his thoughts for
years now—Miss Lucie Manette.

He had loved Lucie Manette ever since his trial.
He had never heard a sound so sweet and dear as
the sound of her voice; he had never seen a face so
tenderly beautiful as hers when she testified on his
behalf at his trial. But he had not yet spoken to
her about his feelings. His uncle's murder had
distracted him and made him feel cautious.

At long last, however, he felt ready to make his
feelings known. One fine summer day, he turned

into the quiet corner in Soho with the thought of speaking his mind to Dr. Manette.

He found the Doctor reading in his armchair at a window. The Doctor, who had now fully regained his energy, looked up with a smile. "Charles Darnay! I rejoice to see you! We have been counting on your return these three or four days past. Mr. Stryver and Sydney Carton were both here yesterday, and both said that you ought to be back soon."

"I am obliged to them for their interest in me," he answered, a little coldly as to them, though very warmly as to the Doctor. "Miss Manette—"

"Is well," said the Doctor, as he stopped short, "and your return will delight us all. She has gone out on some household matters but will soon be home."

"Dr. Manette, I knew she was away from home. I've come to speak to you."

There was a blank silence.

"Yes?" said the Doctor, with a cautious look. "Say what you need to say. Is it about Lucie?"

"She is so wonderful—" began Darnay.

"It is very hard for me to hear her spoken of in that tone of yours, Charles Darnay."

"It is a tone of true admiration and deep love, Dr. Manette!" he said quickly.

There was a blank silence.

"Shall I go on, sir?" asked Darnay.

Another blank.

"Yes, go on."

"You anticipate what I will say, perhaps. Dear Dr. Manette, I love your daughter, dearly. If ever there were love in the world, I love her."

The Doctor sat with his face turned away and his eyes bent on the ground. He dropped his chin in his hands and asked in a **strained**[1] voice, "Have you spoken to Lucie?"

"Never. But I love her. Heaven is my witness that I love her!"

"I believe it," answered her father, mournfully. "I have thought so before now. I believe it."

"But, do not believe," said Darnay quickly, "that I intend to come between you and her. I shall not!"

"You speak so feelingly and so manfully, Charles Darnay, that I thank you with all my heart. Have you any reason to believe that Lucie loves you?"

"No. As yet, none. May I ask, sir, if you think there is another suitor?"

---

[1] **strained**—upset; hoarse.

Her father considered a little before he answered: "You have seen Mr. Carton here yourself. Mr. Stryver is here, too, occasionally. Perhaps they are suitors, although it seems unlikely."

"If I might, Doctor, I'd like to ask you for a favor. If Miss Manette shares with you any feelings of love for me, will you tell her what I have said? Will you tell her that I love her?"

"I give the promise," said the Doctor. "I would never stand in her way against the man she really loves. She is everything to me."

Moved by what the Doctor had said, Darnay continued. "Your confidence in me should be returned with a confidence on my part. My present name is not my own. I wish to tell you what my real name is, and why I am in England."

"Stop!" said the Doctor of Beauvais.

"I wish to tell you, so that I have no secret from you."

"Stop!" The Doctor put his hands to his ears, and then said: "Tell me when I ask you, not now. If it turns out that Lucie does love you, you may tell me on your marriage morning. Otherwise, I don't want to know. Do you promise?"

"Of course."

"Then give me your hand. She will be home directly, and it is better she should not see us together tonight. Go! God bless you!"

A Proposal

If Sydney Carton ever shone anywhere, he certainly never shone in the house of Dr. Manette. He had been there often during the past year, and was usually in a grim and dark mood while visiting. When he cared to talk, he talked well; but more often he was **sullen**[1] and silent.

Although he was a heavy drinker, Sydney never arrived drunk at the Manettes'. He had too much respect for the Doctor and too much admiration for the Doctor's daughter. It was the lovely Lucie, in fact, who drew him to Soho. He thought about her constantly, although he knew

---

[1] **sullen**—gloomily silent.

she would never—could never—return the love of a man such as himself.

Still, on a warm day in August, Sydney found himself once again at the good Doctor's door. He was shown upstairs, and found Lucie at her work, alone. She had never been quite at ease with him, and received him with a little embarrassment as he seated himself near her table. But, looking up at him, she realized that he looked a bit different.

"I fear you are not well, Mr. Carton!"

"No. But the life I lead, Miss Manette, is not **conducive**[2] to health."

"It is a pity, is it not, to lead no better life?"

"God knows it is a shame!"

"Then why not change it?"

Looking gently at him again, she was surprised and saddened to see that there were tears in his eyes. There were tears in his voice too, as he answered: "It is too late for that. I shall never be better than I am. I shall sink lower, and be worse."

She had never seen him this way, and she was very worried.

"Pray forgive me, Miss Manette. I've become emotional even before I've said what I want to say. Will you listen to me?"

---

[2] **conducive**—contributing toward or helping toward.

"Of course, Mr. Carton," she said nervously.

"I know it is impossible, Miss Manette, for you to love me. I am a drunken, wasted creature. I know very well that you can have no tenderness for me, and I ask for none."

"But without it, Mr. Carton, can I help you to a better life? Can I steer you to a better course? Can I help you stop the drinking, the card-playing, the late nights? Can I help you find someone to love who will love you in return?"

"No, Miss Manette. If you will listen just a little more; everything you might ever do for me is done. I wish you to know that you have been the last dream of my soul. At times, I thought that I could become a better man. You inspired these thoughts in me. But I realize now that I can't. I have given up the fight."

> "At times, I thought that I could become a better man. You inspired these thoughts in me. But I realize now that I can't."

"O, Mr. Carton, think again! Try again!"

"The only good that I am capable of now, Miss Manette, I have come here to do. The remembrance that I opened my heart to you is all that I have left. I promise you that if at any time it is in my power to help you, I will do so. I will help you, or a life you love. Do you understand?"[3]

"Yes, of course," she said quietly, although she was not sure that she did.

"Please respect my confidence, and tell no one of our conversation."

"Mr. Carton," she answered, after a pause, "the secret is yours, not mine; and I promise to respect it."

"Thank you. And again, God bless you. For you, and for anyone dear to you, I would do anything. I would embrace any sacrifice for you and for those dear to you. O Miss Manette, please remember this! When you think of me, know that I am a man who would give his life to keep you and those you love free from harm."

---

[3] This statement will be important later in the book.

The Honest Tradesman

Mr. Jerry Cruncher and his child sat one day on their stools in front of Tellson's. The streets were quiet until—

"Look father! It's a buryin'," cried Young Jerry. "Hooray!"

"Quick! Get atop of that there seat, and look at the crowd," the father responded.

His son obeyed, and the crowd approached.

Funerals always interested Mr. Cruncher. "Who is it that's dead?" he asked a passerby.

"Who is it that's dead?" he asked a passerby. The man replied that it was a spy by the name of Roger Cly.

The man replied that it was a **spy**[1] by the name of Roger Cly.

"Was he a spy?" asked Mr. Cruncher.

"He was an Old Bailey spy," answered the man.

"Why, to be sure!" exclaimed Jerry, recalling that he had seen Roger Cly testify at the Charles Darnay trial.

With some noise, the funeral procession passed by. Mr. Cruncher followed along and watched as they buried the casket. After the mourners had gone, he stood staring at the recently dug grave.

Later that night, Jerry said to his son, "I'm goin' fishing."

"Your fishing rod often gets rather rusty and dirty; don't it, father?" Young Jerry asked slyly.

"Never you mind."

"Will you bring any fish home, father? You never seem to."

"Never you mind again."

With that, he opened a locked cupboard, and brought forth a sack, a crowbar of convenient size, a rope and chain, and other fishing tackle of that nature. Then he turned out the light and went out.

Young Jerry, who had only pretended to go off to bed, followed close behind. He was determined to find out more about his father's fishing trips.

---

[1] **spy**—informer.

After a half hour of walking, Young Jerry was surprised to find that his father had led them to a graveyard. His father and another man, who had been waiting there, pulled out their equipment and began to fish.

They fished with a shovel, at first. Then they fished with a pick. Finally they had what seemed like a bite. The two men were bent almost double with the strain of lifting something heavy. Young Jerry knew what it would be. The two men had fished for a coffin, and were about to wrench it open. Unable to watch for another second, Young Jerry ran straight home, imagining the coffin was running after him, bolt upright, upon its narrow end.

The next morning, Jerry Cruncher was in a foul temper. His hands were more rusty than usual, and he would barely say a word.

"Father," said Young Jerry, as they walked along to Tellson's, "what's a resurrection-man?"[2]

---

[2] resurrection-man—another name for a grave-robber, one who digs up coffins after they've been buried in order to steal jewels and other valuables. Some grave-robbers would also steal corpses from the coffins in order to sell them to colleges and universities for medical study.

Mr. Cruncher looked at the boy. "Well! Hmm. He's a tradesman."

"What's his goods, father?" asked Young Jerry.

"His goods," said Mr. Cruncher, after turning it over in his mind, "is a branch of scientific goods."

"Persons' bodies, ain't it, father?" asked the lively boy.

"I believe it is something of that sort," said Mr. Cruncher.

"Oh, father, I should so like to be a resurrection-man when I'm quite growed!"

Mr. Cruncher was soothed and flattered. "That will depend on your talents. Be careful to develop your talents. Be careful to develop your talents, and never say no more than you can help to nobody." Young Jerry, thus encouraged, went on a few yards ahead of his father. Mr. Cruncher added to himself: "Jerry, you honest tradesman, there's hopes for that boy. He may be a blessing to you after all!"

Knitting

It was well past five o'clock when two dusty men passed through the streets of St. Antoine. One of the men was Monsieur Defarge; the other was a mender of roads in a blue cap. Tired and thirsty, the two entered the wine shop.

"Good day, gentlemen!" said Monsieur Defarge.

This greeting elicited an answering chorus of "Good day!"

"My wife," said Defarge aloud, addressing Madame Defarge. "I have traveled certain miles with this good mender of roads, called Jacques. I met him—by accident—a day and a half's journey out of Paris. He is a good man, this mender of roads, called Jacques. Give him a drink, my wife!"

Two men got up and went out. Madame Defarge set wine before the mender of roads, who tipped his blue cap to the company, and drank. In the breast of his blouse he carried some coarse dark bread. He ate this between sips. A third man got up and went out. Defarge refreshed himself with a cup of wine. He looked at no one, and no one now looked at him; not even Madame Defarge, who had taken up her knitting and was at work.

"Have you finished your meal, friend?" he asked the mender of roads.

"Yes, thank you."

"Come, then! You shall see the apartment that I said you could occupy."

Out of the wine shop into the street, out of the street into a courtyard, out of the courtyard up a steep staircase, out of the staircase into a garret— the garret where a white-haired man once sat on a low bench making shoes.

No white-haired man was there now; but the same three men who had just left the wine shop were there. Defarge closed the door carefully, and then spoke in a subdued voice: "Jacques One, Jacques Two, Jacques Three! This is the witness I met by appointment. As I am Jacques Four, he will be Jacques Five. He will tell you his story. Speak, Jacques Five!"

The man in the blue cap cleared his throat and began. "About a year ago, I saw a man hanging underneath the carriage of the Marquis. He was, as I told the Marquis, tall as a specter."

"You should have said short as a dwarf," returned Jacques Two.

"But what did I know? To continue, the authorities have been searching for this tall man for months. They believe that it was he who murdered the Marquis St. Evrémonde.

"Now, just the other day, I was at work upon the hillside when I saw six soldiers. In the midst of them was a tall man with his arms tied to his sides! I stood aside, messieurs,[1] and watched the soldiers and their prisoner pass. When they got quite near, I recognized the tall man, and he recognized me. It was Gaspard, the man whose child had been killed by the Marquis's coach.

> *"It was Gaspard, the man whose child had been killed by the Marquis's coach."*

" 'Come on!' said the chief of soldiers, pointing to the village, 'bring him fast to his tomb!' and they brought him faster.

---

[1] messieurs—the plural of monsieur, which is the title or form of address used for a French man. The English equivalent is mister or sir.

"They brought him into the village and up to the prison. In the morning, with my tools upon my shoulder, I made my way to the prison. There I saw him, high up, behind the bars of an iron cage, all bloody and dusty. He looked at me like a dead man."

Defarge and the three glanced darkly at one another. "Go on, Jacques Five," said Defarge.

"He remained up there in his iron cage for some days. The people in the village whispered that although he was condemned to death, he would not be executed; they said that **petitions**[2] were being presented in Paris showing that he was enraged and mad from the death of his child. They say that a petition was presented to the king himself."

> *"They said that petitions were being presented in Paris showing that he was enraged and mad from the death of his child."*

"Listen all," Jacques One sternly interrupted. "Know that a petition was presented to the king and queen. It did no good."

---

[2] **petitions**—formal requests, usually signed by a number of people, addressed to those in power, asking for a favor, right, or mercy.

After a moment, the mender of roads continued his story. "At length, on Sunday night when all the village was asleep, the soldiers came down from the prison. Workmen dug, workmen hammered, soldiers laughed and sang; in the morning, by the fountain, there was a **gallows**[3] forty feet high.

"In the morning, all the people in the village gathered there. At midday, we heard the roll of drums. Soldiers marched the prisoner into the square. He was bound as before, and in his mouth was a gag—tied so, with a tight string, making him look almost as if he laughed. On the top of the gallows was a knife, blade upwards, with its point in the air. He was hanged there forty feet high— and has been left hanging, ever since, poisoning the water.

"That's all of my story. I left at sunset (as I had been warned to do), and I walked on that night and half the next day, until I met (as I was warned I should) this **comrade**.[4] With him, I came on, now riding and now walking, through the rest of yesterday and through last night. And here you see me!"

---

[3] **gallows**—wooden framework from which criminals are hanged.

[4] **comrade**—a fellow member of a group or political party.

After a gloomy silence, Defarge said, "Good! You have told your story faithfully. Will you wait for us a little outside the door?"

"Very willingly," said the mender of roads.

After he left, the four remaining Jacques looked at each other.

"Should we register the château and all the race in Madame's knitting?" demanded Number One.

"The château and all the race," agreed Defarge. "Extermination."

The first Jacques, who had a hungry, craving air, said, "Magnificent!" and began gnawing on a finger.

"Then so be it," said Defarge. "He will be added to the register. And as you know, gentlemen, it is impossible to erase one letter of a name or crime from the knitted register of Madame Defarge."

Still Knitting

An evening or two later, the Defarges, husband and wife, walked in the night air. Madame Defarge spoke to her husband: "Say then, my husband, what has **thee**[1] heard from Jacques of the police?"

"Very little. There is another spy coming to our quarter. There may be many more for all that he can say, but he knows of only one."

"Eh well!" said Madame Defarge, raising her eyebrows with a cool business air. "It is necessary to register him. What do they call the man?"

"He is English. His name is John Barsad."

"John Barsad," repeated Madame, after murmuring it once to herself. "Good. His appearance. Is it known?"

---

[1] **thee**—an intimate form of "you."

"Age, about forty years; height, about five feet nine; black hair; complexion dark; generally, rather handsome; eyes dark, face thin, long, and sallow; nose **aquiline**,[2] but not straight; expression, therefore, **sinister**."[3]

"Eh my faith. It is a portrait!" said Madame, laughing. "He shall be registered tomorrow."

They turned into the wine shop, which was closed (for it was midnight). The night was hot, and the shop, closed shut and surrounded by so foul a neighborhood, was ill-smelling.

"You are tired," said Madame, as she counted the coins from the day's sales.

"I am a little tired," her husband acknowledged.

"You are a little depressed, too," said Madame. "You must have faith."

"But my dear!" began Defarge.

"But my dear!" repeated Madame, nodding firmly; "but my dear! Why are you faint of heart tonight, my dear?"

"Well, then," said Defarge, "the Revolution.[4] It is a long time in coming."

---

[2] **aquiline**—curved or hooked like an eagle's beak.

[3] **sinister**—suggesting or threatening evil.

[4] Revolution—The French Revolution (1789-99) violently transformed France from a country ruled by a monarchy with a rigid class structure into a modern nation in which the power was held by the middle classes.

"It is a long time," repeated his wife; "and when is it not a long time? **Vengeance**[5] and **retribution**[6] require a long time; it is the rule."

"Yes, a long time, I suppose," said Defarge.

"But when we are ready, when everything is in place, we will grind to pieces everything before us. In the meantime, we are always preparing. Nothing that we do is done in vain. I believe, with all my soul, that we shall see the triumph. But, even if we do not, show me the neck of an aristocrat and **tyrant**,[7] and I will—"

"Hold!" cried Defarge. "I too, my dear, will stop at nothing! At nothing!"

The next morning, a man who called himself John Barsad entered the wine shop. After asking for a glass of wine, he turned to Monsieur Defarge and said, "You and I have friends in common, Monsieur Defarge."

"Indeed?" said Defarge, cautiously.

"Yes, indeed. I speak of Doctor Manette. When Doctor Manette was released, he was delivered to you, his old servant."

"Yes," said Defarge briefly.

---

[5] **Vengeance**—punishment in return for a wrong committed; revenge.

[6] **retribution**—repayment in the form of a punishment. Madame Defarge is a strong woman who is ruled by hate.

[7] **tyrant**—a ruler who exercises power in a harsh, cruel manner.

"It was to you," said the spy, "that his daughter came; and it was from your care that his daughter took him, accompanied by a neat, brown monsieur in a little wig—Monsieur Lorry, of the Bank of Tellson and Company."

"Yes," repeated Defarge.

"I have known Dr. Manette and his daughter in England," said the spy.

"Yes?" said Defarge.

"You don't hear much from them now?" said the spy.

"No," said Defarge.

"In effect," Madame struck in, looking up from her work, "we never hear about them at all."

"Perfectly so, Madame," replied the spy. "She is going to be married."

"Yes?" responded Madame.

"Yes, Miss Manette is going to be married. But not to an Englishman; to one who, like herself, is French by birth. And, Madame, it is a curious thing—she is going to marry the nephew of Monsieur the Marquis, who is, of course, the present Marquis. He lives unknown in England; he is no Marquis there. He is Mr. Charles Darnay."

Madame Defarge knitted steadily, but the information had an effect upon her husband. His hand shook, and the spy must have noticed.

"Can it be true," said Defarge, in a low voice after Barsad left, "what he has said of Mademoiselle Manette?"

"Perhaps," returned Madame.

"If it is—" Defarge began, and stopped.

"If it is?" repeated his wife.

"If it is true, I hope for her sake that her husband stays out of France."

And still Madame Defarge knitted, adding an additional name to her register: Charles St. Evrémonde, known in England as Charles Darnay.

BOOK TWO

A Wedding

Never did the sun rise with a brighter glory than on the blessed morning of Lucie's wedding day. She and her father, who had been up the whole night, talked quietly as the sun rose.

"I am very happy today, dear father, because I love Charles very much. But I will tell you once again that I shall never leave you. You and I will be together always."

He hugged her, and humbly thanked heaven for having given her to him.

Later in the morning, a small but jolly group assembled in the front room of the house in Soho. Mr. Lorry, Mrs. Pross, and Lucie all fussed about each other, anxious to get started for the church.

The door of the Doctor's study opened, and out came Dr. Manette with Charles Darnay. The Doctor was deadly pale, and yet he gave his arm to his daughter, and took her downstairs to the carriage that Mr. Lorry had hired in honor of the day. The rest followed in another carriage, and soon, in a neighboring church, Charles Darnay and Lucie Manette were happily married.

> *The door of the Doctor's study opened, and out came Dr. Manette with Charles Darnay.*

After the service, it was time to say farewell. It was a hard parting, though it was not for long, as their wedding trip was to last just nine days. Still, Lucie's father had to disengage himself from Lucie's arms, saying, "Take her, Charles! She is yours!"

And then she was gone.

Later that night, at the house in Soho, Mr. Lorry and Miss Pross were startled by the low sound of knocking.

"Good God!" Mr. Lorry said with a start. "What's that?"

Miss Pross, with a terrified face, was at his ear. "O me, O me! All is lost!" she cried. "What will I tell Ladybird? He doesn't recognize me, and is back to making shoes!"

Mr. Lorry said what he could to calm her, and went himself into the Doctor's room. The bench was turned towards the light, as it had been when he had seen the shoemaker at his work before, and his head was bent down, and he was very busy.

"Dr. Manette. My dear friend, Dr. Manette!"

The Doctor looked at him for a moment—half inquiringly, half as if he were angry at being spoken to—and bent over his work again.

"Dr. Manette. Look at me."

He obeyed, in the old mechanical manner, without pausing in his work.

"You know me, my dear friend?"

The Doctor would not say a word although he sometimes looked up with a confused or surprised expression. Two things at once impressed themselves on Mr. Lorry, as important above all others; the first, that this—this collapse—must be kept secret from Lucie; the second, that it must be kept secret from all who knew him.

Accordingly, Mr. Lorry sent word out that the Doctor was not well, and required a few days of rest. Miss Pross wrote to Lucie that her father had been called away on a case.

For nine days, Mr. Lorry and Miss Pross kept a silent watch over the Doctor. He never spoke a word in all this time. Instead, he sat busily making shoes and was growing dreadfully skilled and expert at it. The time went very slowly, and Mr. Lorry's heart grew heavier and heavier.

On the tenth morning of the watch, Mr. Lorry was startled to see that the shoemaker's bench and tools were put aside again, and that the Doctor himself sat reading at the window. He was in his usual morning dress, and his face, though still very pale, was calm and attentive.

What had happened? Miss Pross and Mr. Lorry anxiously conferred. They could find no reason for the change in the Doctor, but realized that he was back to his old self again. They decided to say nothing, but vowed to keep a careful watch.

One day, Mr. Lorry consulted with Dr. Manette about a curious case. A dear friend had received a severe shock from which he had recovered. But then there was a **relapse**[1] and Mr. Lorry's friend resumed an old activity connected with the shock. Mr. Lorry said, "I am a man of business, unfit to deal with such matters. What can I do for my friend?"

"I think it is probable," said the Doctor, "that the relapse was not a total surprise to your friend."

---

[1] **relapse**—return of an illness or old activity after a painful recovery.

"Would he remember what took place in the relapse?" asked Mr. Lorry.

The Doctor shook his head, "Not at all. But as to the future, I should hope the worst was over."

"The occupation he resumed, we will call— blacksmith's work. It is a pity that he should keep it by him."

The Doctor shaded his forehead with his hand and beat his foot nervously on the ground.

"You see, it is such an old companion," said the Doctor.

"I would not keep it," said Mr. Lorry. "Come! Give me your authority, like a dear good man."

"I approve of it, but do not take it away while he is present; let him miss his old companion after he has been away."

Three days later, Mr. Lorry and Miss Pross put the Doctor in a coach bound for a reunion with Lucie and Charles. The Doctor waved brightly out the window and reminded them to take care of the house.

In the evening, Mr. Lorry went into the Doctor's room with a saw, chisel, and hammer. There, with closed doors, and in a mysterious and guilty manner, Mr. Lorry hacked the shoemaker's bench to pieces.

The Footsteps Approach

When the newly married pair arrived home, the first person who appeared to offer his congratulations was Sydney Carton. He was not improved in habits, or in looks, or in manner; but there was a certain calmness that seemed new to the observation of Charles Darnay.

Carton watched his opportunity of taking Darnay aside, and of speaking to him when no one overheard.

"Mr. Darnay," said Carton, "you know me as a dog who has never done any good, and never will."

"I don't know that you 'never will.'"

"But I do, and you must take my word for it. Well! If you could stand to have such a worthless fellow visit you and Mrs. Darnay at odd times, I ask that you will allow me to come and go, that I might be regarded as a useless piece of furniture, tolerated for its old service. I doubt if I should abuse the permission. It would satisfy me to know that I had it."

"Will you try?"

"That is another way of saying that I am on the footing I indicated. I thank you, Darnay."

They shook hands upon it, and Carton turned away.

When he had gone, Charles Darnay spoke of their conversation and told Miss Pross, the Doctor, and Mr. Lorry that Sydney Carton was reckless and bound for trouble. Darnay did not mean to be hard on the man, but he felt he must speak the truth.

Later, he joined his wife in their room. He found her with a look of concentration upon her face.

"We are thoughtful tonight!" said Darnay, drawing his arm about her.

"Yes, dearest Charles, we are rather thoughtful tonight, for we have something on our mind."

"What is it, my Lucie?"

"Will you promise not to press one question on me, if I beg you not to ask it?"

"What will I not promise for my love."

> *"What will I not promise for my love."*

"I think, Charles, poor Mr. Carton deserves more kindness and respect than you expressed for him tonight."

"Indeed? Why so?"

"That is what you are not to ask me. But I think—I know—he does."

"If you know it, it is enough. What would you have me do, my sweet?"

"I would ask you, dearest, to be very generous with him always, and very lenient on his faults when he is not there. I would ask you to believe that he has a heart he very, very seldom reveals, and that there are deep wounds in it. My dear, I have seen it bleeding."

"It is painful to me," said Charles Darnay, quite astonished, "to think that I have done him any wrong."

"My husband, I am sure that he is capable of good things, gentle things, even **magnanimous**[1] things." She looked so beautiful in the purity of her

---

[1] **magnanimous**—courageously noble.

faith in this lost man that her husband could have looked at her for hours.

"And, O my dearest love," she urged, "remember how strong we are in our happiness, and how weak he is in his misery!"

The plea touched his heart. "I will always remember it, dear heart! I will remember it as long as I live. God bless you for your sweet compassion!"

Life was pleasant for the young newlyweds. They lived happily with Dr. Manette and Miss Pross in the same little house in Soho. Lucie, who was content with her life and her work, ran an efficient, happy household. Busy as she was, however, Lucie always had time to listen to the echo of the footsteps outside on the street. Usually the footsteps had a lively, cheerful sound. Every once in a while, though, she would hear something in the footsteps that frightened her. She would listen as intently as she could, wondering if the footsteps would approach her door or pass by. In those early years, the footsteps always passed by, and she was grateful.

The time passed, and soon her little Lucie was born. Then, among the footsteps, there was the tread of little Lucie's tiny feet and the sound of her prattling words. Little Lucie's brother was born soon after, although he was not as strong as his sister, and was called to heaven much too quickly.

Some half dozen times a year, Lucie would hear the footsteps of Sydney Carton approaching her door. He never came drunk. Each time, Lucie and Charles welcomed him with open arms, and made a place for him in their little family. Carton was the first stranger to whom little Lucie held out her chubby arms, and he kept his place with her as she grew.

Mr. Stryver shouldered his way through the law, like some great engine forcing itself through rough water, and dragged his friend, Carton, in his wake. Stryver had married a widow with property and three boys. Now and again, Lucie would hear the echo of Mr. Stryver's footsteps, followed by the clump and gallop of his three eager sons.

In the year that Lucie was six, the echo of the footsteps began to change. There were other echoes from a distance that had a **menacing**[2] sound, an awful sound of a rising storm at sea that frightened Lucie badly. The great storm of protest in France,

2 **menacing**—threatening.

which had begun years before, seemed to come closer, closer, and closer to the little house in Soho.

On a night in mid-July, 1789, Mr. Lorry came in late from Tellson's, and sat himself down by Lucie and her husband. It was a hot, wild night, and they were all three reminded of the old Sunday night when they had looked at the lightning from the same place.

"I began to think," said Mr. Lorry, pushing his flaxen wig back, "that I should have to stay the night at Tellson's. We have been so full of business all day that we have not known what to do first, or which way to turn. There is such an uneasiness in Paris. Our French customers have been frantically sending their property to us in England."

"Things will become much worse before they take a turn for the better."

"That has a bad look," said Darnay.

"I know that, to be sure," agreed Mr. Lorry. "Things will become much worse before they take a turn for the better.

"The footsteps are very numerous and very loud tonight, are they not?"

"I hear them in my sleep, it seems," responded Lucie quietly.

The Bastille

In the Saint Antoine district of Paris, an angry roar rose from the people. A forest of naked arms struggled in the air like shriveled tree branches in the winter wind. All hands clutched weapons. **Muskets**[1] were distributed—and so were bars of iron and wood, knives, axes, **pikes**,[2] and any other weapon imaginable. People who could find nothing else set themselves with bleeding hands to force stones and bricks out of their places in walls. Every pulse and heart in Saint Antoine beat feverishly. Everyone held life as of no account, and was crazy with a passionate willingness to sacrifice it.

---

[1] **Muskets**—shoulder-guns.
[2] **pikes**—long spears.

"Keep near to me, Jacques Three," cried Defarge, "and you, Jacques One and Two, watch over as many of these patriots as you can. Where is my wife?"

"Eh, well! Here you see me!" said Madame, composed as ever, but not knitting today. In Madame's right hand was an ax, and in her waist-band were a pistol and a cruel knife.

"Where do you go, my wife?"

"I go," said Madame, "with you at present. You shall see me at the head of the women, by-and-by."

"Come, then!" cried Defarge, in a **resounding**[3] voice. "Patriots and friends, we are ready for revolution! To the Bastille!"[4]

With a roar that sounded as if all of France had joined in, the living sea of people marched to the Bastille. Alarm bells rang and drums pounded. The attack had begun.

Deep ditches, double drawbridges, massive stone walls, eight great towers, cannons, muskets, fire and smoke—nothing could stop them.

---

[3] **resounding**—loud and strong.

[4] Bastille—a fortress and prison in Paris, seen as a symbol of aristocratic rule in France. During the 1700s, the Bastille was used as a prison and storage facility for guns and munitions. On July 14, 1789, at the beginning of the French Revolution, a mob gathered outside the Bastille and demanded that they be given the guns and gunpowder stored within its walls. The commander, the Marquis de Launay, refused to surrender, so the mob stormed the building.

For two fierce hours, Defarge worked like a soldier. Deep ditches, single drawbridge, massive stone walls, eight great towers, cannon, muskets, fire and smoke. One drawbridge down!

"Work, comrades, work! Work, Jacques One, Jacques Two, Jacques One Thousand, Jacques Two Thousand, Jacques Five-and-Twenty Thousand—work!"

"Hear me, women!" cried Madame his wife. "We can kill as well as the men!" With a shrill, thirsty cry, troops of women armed themselves and joined the fight.

Flashing weapons, blazing torches, smoking wagonloads of wet straw, hard work at **barricades**[5] in all directions, shrieks, yells, and curses; but, still the deep ditch, and the single drawbridge, and the massive stone walls, and the eight great towers, and still Defarge of the wine shop at his gun.

A white flag flew within the fortress, and in swept Defarge and his men over the lowered drawbridge, past the massive stone outer walls, in among the eight great towers—the Bastille had surrendered! Everywhere was **tumult**[6] and **jubilation**[7].

---

[5] **barricades**—barriers.

[6] **tumult**—din; uproar.

[7] **jubilation**—rejoicing.

"The prisoners!"

"The records!"

"The secret cells!"

"The instruments of torture!"

"The prisoners! Free them!"

"Where is One Hundred and Five, North Tower?" Defarge demanded of a **turnkey**.[8] "Show me now!"

"Come this way, Monsieur."

Through gloomy vaults where the light of day had never shone, past dark dens and cages, up narrow flights of steps traveled Defarge, the turnkey, and Jacques Three.

The turnkey stopped at a low door, put a key in a clashing lock, swung the door slowly open, and said, as they all bent their heads and passed in: "One Hundred and Five, North Tower!"

There was a small, heavily barred, open window high in the wall, with a stone screen before it, so that the sky could be only seen by stooping low and looking up. There was a small chimney with a heap of old, feathery wood ashes on the hearth. There was a stool and table, and a straw

---

[8] **turnkey**—the keeper of the keys in a prison; a jailer.

bed. There were the four blackened walls, with a rusted iron ring in one of them.

"Pass that torch slowly along these walls, so that I may see them," said Defarge to the turnkey.

The man obeyed, and Defarge followed the light closely with his eyes.

"Stop—Look here, Jacques!"

"A.M.!" croaked Jacques Three, as he read greedily.

"Alexandre Manette," said Defarge in his ear, following the letters with his forefinger. "And here he wrote 'a poor physician.' Here! Give that crowbar to me!"

He turned to the worm-eaten stool and table and beat them to pieces in a few blows. "Hold the light higher!" he said angrily to the turnkey. "Look among those fragments with care, Jacques. And see! Here is my knife," throwing it to him, "rip open that bed, and search the straw. Hold the light higher, you!"

Defarge crawled upon the hearth, and, peering up the chimney, poked at its sides with the crowbar and worked at the iron grating across it. In a few minutes, some mortar and dust came dropping down.

"Nothing in the wood, and nothing in the straw, Jacques?"

"Nothing."

"Then we will burn it all. Light a fire, you!"

"Then we will burn it all. Light a fire, you!"

The turnkey fired the little pile, which blazed high and hot. Then the three returned to the courtyard and joined the flood of rioting, unpitying faces once again.

Now, heaven keep those feet far out of the life of Lucie Darnay! For they are headlong, mad, and dangerous.

The Fire Rises

For one week, the people of Saint Antoine cele-
brated their victory at the Bastille. Madame Defarge
sat knitting and watching with approval as the
people **exulted**[1] in their power to destroy. One of
her sisterhood knitted beside her. This woman—
who was the short, plump wife of a starved grocer
and the mother of two children—had earned the
name of The Vengeance.

"Hark!" said The Vengeance. "Listen, then!
Who comes?"

"It is Defarge," said Madame. "Silence, patriots!"

---

[1] **exulted**—rejoiced.

Defarge came in breathless, pulled off a red cap he wore, and looked around him.

"Listen to him!" said Madame again. "Say then, my husband. What is it?"

"News from the other world! Does everybody here recall old Foulon, the tax collector of the Marquis who told starving people to eat grass and died at the start of the Revolution?"

"Everybody!" from all throats.

"The news is of him. He is among us! He is not dead! He feared us so much—and with reason—that he faked his own death, and had a grand mock funeral. But they have

> *"The news is of him. He is among us! He is not dead!"*

found him alive, hiding in the country, and have brought him in. I have seen him, on his way to the Hôtel de Ville,[2] a prisoner. Patriots!" he continued, in a determined voice, "are we ready?"

Instantly Madame Defarge's knife was in her waistband; the drum was beating in the streets, and The Vengeance, uttering terrific shrieks, was tearing from house to house, rousing the women.

---

[2] Hôtel de Ville—City Hall.

The Defarges, husband and wife, The Vengeance, and Jacques Three led the way. Onward they marched, through fields and forests, until they had arrived at the Hôtel de Ville, where Foulon, closely guarded, was bound with ropes with a bunch of grass tied on his back.

The crowd surged upon the prisoner; the guards were no match for the men and women of Saint Antoine. After a short, bloody brawl, they had him. Saint Antoine had got him!

"Bring him out! Bring him to the lamp!" was the cry.

They dragged him, on his knees, on his back. He panted and begged for mercy and screamed in agony. He was hauled to the nearest street corner where one of the fatal lamps swung. Once, he went **aloft**,[3] and the rope broke, and they caught him shrieking; twice, he went aloft, and the rope broke, and they caught him shrieking; then, the rope was merciful, and held him, and his head was soon upon a pike, with grass in his mouth, and the people of Saint Antoine began to dance.

It was almost morning when Monsieur Defarge said to Madame, hoarsely, "At last it is come, my dear!"

"Eh well!" returned Madame. "Almost."

---

[3] **aloft**—far above the earth; high up.

After the old tax collector, Foulon, was hanged, there was a change in the country village in the hollow. The villagers were stronger, though they were still hungry. They were more powerful, though they were still scrawny and underfed. The Revolution had made them bold, and they were ready to fight. No enemy was too great; no cause was too small.

A new cause came upon the village one summer afternoon in July. On that day, a tall, shaggy-haired man walked up the hill toward the village and approached the mender of roads, who was out repairing a rut in the road to the village.

"How goes it, Jacques?" the man said.

"All is well, Jacques."

"Show me the château of the Marquis, may he rot in hell!" said the traveler then, moving to the top of the hill.

"See it," returned the mender of roads, with an extended finger. "About two leagues[4] beyond the top of that hill above the village."

"When do you stop work? I have walked two nights without resting. Will you waken me?"

---

[4] A league is equal to about three miles. The mender of roads is telling the man that the château is approximately six miles away.

When the roadmender woke him he said, "Good. Two leagues beyond the summit of the hill?"

"Yes."

The mender of roads went home and told the village what was to happen. The night deepened, and the village watched. Soon, the château of the Marquis began to make itself strangely visible by some light of its own. Then, a flickering streak played behind the architecture of the front. Then it soared higher and grew broader and brighter. Soon, from **a score**[5] of the great windows, flames burst forth, and the château was engulfed in flames.

In the village in the hollow and in the surrounding villages, the people rang bells, put candles in each window, and called out in joy. Smaller fires dotted the countryside, east, west, north, and south. Soon, smaller fires joined together and made larger and larger fires, until it seemed that all of France was burning.

---

[5] **a score**—twenty.

A Plea

The fire that burned the countryside of France could not cross the Channel to England. Still, the French Revolution made itself felt in other ways. By 1792, the French court no longer existed. It had gone forever. The aristocracy had scattered to foreign lands. Those who could not escape were hanged or burned or imprisoned. Small groups of men and women—such as the men and women of Saint Antoine—controlled the country.

At Tellson's, people gathered to hear the news from France. On a steaming, misty afternoon, Mr. Lorry sat at his desk, and Charles Darnay stood leaning on it, talking with him in a low voice. Mr. Lorry had revealed to Charles that he was to be sent to oversee the branch of Tellson's in Paris.

"I wish I were going myself," said Charles Darnay, somewhat restlessly.

"Indeed!" exclaimed Mr. Lorry. "You wish you were going yourself? And you a Frenchman born?"

"My dear Mr. Lorry, it is because I am a Frenchman that the Revolution has passed through my mind often. I can't help thinking that because I understand the misery of the French peasants, I might be able to persuade them to restrain themselves. Their revolution is for the common good, but their methods are so **barbaric**,[1] so bloody—"

"The truth is, my dear Charles, that France is far too dangerous a place for a man such as yourself, with a wife and a child to care for," interrupted Mr. Lorry. "I must leave tonight, because of the urgency of my business. Please extend my farewells to Lucie and the others."

"Do you take no one with you?"

"I intend to take Jerry Cruncher. Nobody will suspect Jerry of being anything but an English bulldog. He will protect me."

Just then, a Tellson's House messenger approached Mr. Lorry and laid a soiled and unopened letter before him. Did Mr. Lorry know the person to whom it was addressed? The messenger laid the letter down so close to Darnay

---

[1] **barbaric**—uncivilized.

that he saw the address—especially because it was his own right name. The address, turned into English, read:

"Very pressing. To Monsieur **heretofore**[2] the Marquis St. Evrémonde, of France. In the care of Messrs. Tellson and Co., Bankers, London, England."

On the morning of Charles Darnay's wedding, Dr. Manette had made one urgent request to him: that the secret of this name should be kept secret between them. No one else knew that Darnay was St. Evrémonde. Even his own wife had no suspicion of the fact.

"No," said Mr. Lorry, in reply to the messenger; "I have asked everyone here, and no one can tell me where this gentleman is to be found."

As the Bank was closing, there was a crowd of people moving back and forth by Mr. Lorry's desk. He held the letter out inquiringly; one man looked at it, and then another, and another and another. All had something **disparaging**[3] to say, in French or in English, concerning the Marquis who was not to be found.

---

[2] **heretofore**—previously, up to now.
[3] **disparaging**—disrespectful, belittling.

*"It is the nephew,
I believe, of
the Marquis who
was murdered,"
said one.*

"It is the nephew, I believe, of the Marquis who was murdered," said one. "Happy to say I never knew him."

"He is a coward who abandoned his post some years ago," said another.

"He opposed the last Marquis, abandoned the estates when he inherited them, and left them to be ruined by the peasants. They will pay him back now, I hope, as he deserves."

Darnay, unable to restrain himself any longer, touched Mr. Lorry on the shoulder, and said: "I know the fellow."

"Do you, by Jupiter?" said Mr. Stryver, who was standing nearby. "I am sorry for it. Did you hear what he did? This is a man who abandoned his property to the vilest scum of the earth. Those who control his land are murderers of the worst kind."

Mindful of the secret, Darnay with great difficulty controlled himself, and said: "You may not understand the gentleman."

"Will you take charge of the letter?" said Mr. Lorry to Darnay. "You know where to deliver it?"

"I do. Do you start for Paris from here?"

"From here, at eight."

"I will come back, to see you off."

Very ill at ease with himself, Darnay made his way out the door, opened the letter, and read it. These were its contents:

Prison of the Abbey, Paris
June 21, 1792

MONSIEUR HERETOFORE THE MARQUIS,

After having long been in danger of my life at the hands of people in the village, I have been seized, with great violence, and brought to Paris. My house has been destroyed, and I have suffered a great deal.

The crime for which I am imprisoned, Monsieur heretofore the Marquis, and for which I shall be summoned before the **Tribunal**,[4] and shall lose my life (without your generous help), is, they tell me, treason against the majesty of the people. They say that I have acted against them for an **emigrant**.[5] I've told them I have acted on their behalf, according to your commands, but they do not believe me. I have collected no rent and no taxes for quite

---

[4] **Tribunal**—court of justice.
[5] **emigrant**—person who has left one country or region to settle in another.

some time, but they ignore this fact. Their only response is that I have acted for an emigrant, and where is that emigrant?

Ah! Most gracious Monsieur heretofore the Marquis, where is that emigrant? I cry in my sleep: Where is he? Will you not come to deliver me? I send my cry across the sea, hoping it may perhaps reach your ears through the great Bank of Tellson. For the love of heaven, of justice, of generosity, of the honor of your name, I ask you to help me. My only fault is that I have been true to you. Oh Monsieur heretofore the Marquis, I pray you, be true to me!

Your honest tax collector,
"GABELLE"

Gabelle's plea struck a chord with Darnay. Gabelle had been a faithful servant all these years, and now he was to be murdered for it!

Darnay knew that because of his hatred for his uncle and his shame of his family name, he had acted imperfectly. He had given up his estate and property, but he had done it hurriedly. He knew that he ought to have carefully worked it out and supervised it, and that he had meant to do it, and that it had never been done.

Instead, he had left written instructions that Monsieur Gabelle was to spare the people, to give them what little there was to give. Clearly, the people had misunderstood. Clearly, he would have to go to Paris. He would go to help Gabelle, an innocent prisoner in danger of execution.

As he walked to and fro with his resolution made, he realized that neither Lucie nor her father must know of his decision until he was gone. They must be spared the pain of parting.

He walked to and fro, with thoughts very busy, until it was time to return to Tellson's and take leave of Mr. Lorry. As soon as he arrived in Paris, he would present himself to this old friend, but he must say nothing of his plans now.

"I have delivered that letter," said Charles Darnay to Mr. Lorry, when he arrived back at the Bank. "Would you be able to deliver a response once you arrive in Paris?"

"Of course," said Mr. Lorry, "if it is not dangerous."

"Not at all. Though it is to a prisoner in the Abbey. His name is Gabelle."

"Gabelle. And what is the message to the unfortunate Gabelle in prison?"

"Simply, 'that he has received the letter, and will come.'"

Charles helped Mr. Lorry wrap himself in a number of coats and cloaks, and then watched as his coach pulled away.

That night—it was the fourteenth of August—Charles sat up late and wrote two letters; one was to Lucie, explaining the strong obligation he was under to go to Paris. The other was to the Doctor, giving Lucie and their dear child to his care.

On the fifteenth of August, he left all that was dear on earth behind him, and began his journey to Paris.

THE END OF BOOK TWO

The Track
of a Storm

In Secret

Darnay's journey to Paris was slow and uncomfortable. Under the New Republic, the roads had fallen apart, and the new system of border crossings was a nightmare of delays, questionings, and frustrations. A very few miles into France, Charles began to understand that he would never be allowed to leave again until he was declared a good citizen by the new authorities in Paris. He understood all too well the citizen-patriots' motto of "Republic One and Indivisible, of Liberty, Equality, Fraternity, or Death."

One night he was awakened by an official and three armed patriots in rough red caps who sat on the bed. "I am going to send you to Paris, under an escort," said the official. They travelled at night. By the time he reached the town of Beauvais, Charles was exhausted and very shaken. He had been treated badly along the way, and things were no better in the town. He was alarmed by the many voices that called out, "Down with the emigrant!"

"I am no emigrant, my friends! Don't you see that I am here, in France, of my own will?"[1]

"You are a cursed emigrant," cried a blacksmith, "and you are a cursed aristocrat!"

"You are a cursed emigrant," cried a **blacksmith**,[2] "and you are a cursed aristocrat!"

A postmaster interrupted and said soothingly, "Let him be; let him be! He will be judged in Paris."

"Judged!" repeated the blacksmith, swinging his hammer. "Ay! and condemned as a traitor." At this, the crowd roared approval.

"Friends, you deceive yourselves, or you are deceived. I am no traitor."

"He lies!" cried another man. "He is a traitor since the **decree**.[3] His life is not his own!"

---

[1] Of course, the peasants don't realize that Darnay gave up his title and land many years ago. They blame him for their poverty and hunger, since they are working land owned by the Evrémonde family.

[2] **blacksmith**—person who works in iron, including the making of horseshoes.

[3] **decree**—an order that has the force of law.

"What is this decree that the man spoke of?" Darnay asked the postmaster.

"It is a decree for selling the property of emigrants. Everybody says it is but one of several, and that there will be others—if there are not already—banishing all emigrants, and condemning all to death who return. That is what he meant when he said your life was not your own."

"But there are no such decrees yet?"

"What do I know?" said the postmaster, shrugging his shoulders, "there may be, or there will be. It is all the same."

Darnay and his escort continued their ride in silence. At last they reached the wall of Paris. The barrier was closed and strongly guarded when they rode up to it.

"Where are the papers of this prisoner?" demanded a grim-looking man, who was summoned by the guard.

"I am not a prisoner. I am a French citizen," responded Darnay.

"Where," repeated the man, ignoring him, "are the papers of this prisoner?"

Darnay's escort handed the papers, including Gabelle's letter, to the man in authority, who looked at them, then looked closely at Darnay, and then left without a word.

After a wait of a half-hour or more, the man returned. Darnay was to accompany him into the guardroom, where another officer was waiting.

"Citizen Defarge," said the officer to Darnay's conductor, "is this the emigrant Evrémonde?"

"This is the man," replied Defarge.

"Your age, Evrémonde?"

"Thirty-seven."

"Married, Evrémonde?"

"Yes."

"Where is your wife, Evrémonde?"

"In England."

"But of course. You are **consigned**,[4] Evrémonde, to the prison of La Force."

"Just heaven!" exclaimed Darnay. "Under what law, and for what offense?"

The officer looked up from his slip of paper for a moment. "We have new laws, Evrémonde, since you were last here." He said it with a hard smile, and went on writing.

"But surely I have the right to—" began Darnay.

"Emigrants have no rights, Evrémonde," interrupted the officer. He handed over a paper to

---

[4] **consigned**—committed.

Defarge with the words "In Secret" written across the front.

Defarge motioned to the prisoner that he must accompany him. The prisoner obeyed, and a guard of two armed patriots attended them.

"Is it you," said Defarge, in a low voice, as they went down the guard-house steps, "who married the daughter of Dr. Manette, once a prisoner in the Bastille?"

"Yes," replied Darnay, looking at him with surprise.

"My name is Defarge, and I keep a wine shop in the district of Saint Antoine. Possibly you have heard of me."

"My wife came to your house to reclaim her father? Yes!"

The word "wife" seemed to serve as a gloomy reminder to Defarge. He said with sudden impatience, "In the name of La Guillotine,[5] why did you come to France?"

---

[5] La Guillotine—the guillotine, a device used for cutting off people's heads, was first used extensively during the French Revolution. It was named for a physician, Joseph Ignace Guillotin (1738-1814), who recommended that all executions be carried out in a uniform, painless way. It became the symbol of the Reign of Terror (1793-94), when thousands of people died under its blade. It remained the principal method of execution in France until capital punishment was abolished there in 1981.

"I have explained. I've come to help a man called Gabelle."

"A poor decision on your part," muttered Defarge.

"Indeed, I am lost here. Can you give me a little help?"

"None." Defarge spoke, always looking straight before him.

"It is of the utmost importance to me that I should be able to communicate to Mr. Lorry of Tellson's Bank the simple fact, without comment, that I have been thrown into the prison of La Force. Will you do that for me?"

"I will do nothing for you," Defarge replied. "My duty is to my country and the people. I am the sworn servant of both, against you. I will do nothing for you."

Without another word, Defarge led his prisoner to La Force.

At the entrance to the prison, Defarge presented his prisoner: "The emigrant Evrémonde."

La Force was a gloomy prison, dark and filthy, and with a horrible smell of foul sleep in it. It is strange how soon the flavor of imprisoned sleep becomes obvious in places that are not cared for. "Come!" said the prison chief, at length taking up his keys, "come with me, emigrant."

Through the dismal prison twilight, Darnay and the prison chief made their way to a large, low chamber that was crowded with prisoners of both sexes.

"In the name of our small group," said a prisoner of courtly appearance, coming forward, "I have the honour of welcoming you to La Force. I hope, good sir, that you are not In Secret?"

> **"I have the honour of welcoming you to La Force. I hope, good sir, that you are not In Secret?"**

"I do not understand the meaning of the term, but I have heard them say so."

"Ah, what a pity! We so much regret it! But take courage; several members of our society have been In Secret, and it has lasted but a short time." Then he added, raising his voice, "I grieve to inform the society—In Secret."

There was a murmur of **commiseration**[6] as Charles Darnay crossed the room to a grated door where the gaoler awaited him, and stepped inside a cell.

"Yours," said the gaoler.

"Why am I confined alone?"

---

[6] **commiseration**—expression of pity or compassion.

"How do I know! The paper said 'In Secret.' This means that you are to stay in a cell alone."

"I can buy pen, ink, and paper?"

"Such are not my orders. You will be visited, and can ask then. At present, you may buy your food, and nothing more."

In the cell was a chair, a table, and a straw mattress covered by crawling insects. As soon as the gaoler left, Darnay began to pace. "Five paces by four-and-a-half; five paces by four-and-a-half; five paces by four-and-a-half," he said over and over to himself, and the roar of the city rose like muffled drums with a swell of voices added to them. "He made shoes, he made shoes, he made shoes." Darnay counted the measurement again, and paced faster, to draw his mind away from shoes. And yet—"He made shoes, he made shoes, he made shoes."

The Grindstone

The Paris branch of Tellson's Bank was in the Saint Germain district of the city. Late one after-noon, at the end of August, Mr. Jarvis Lorry sat in his office at Tellson's, Paris, and considered the changes the Revolution had brought. From a banker's viewpoint, France was a wreck. Many of Tellson's clients had suffered severe setbacks. Each new day at the Bank brought scores of fresh problems.

On this particular afternoon, Mr. Lorry was so intent on his work that he failed to hear his office door open or his visitors approach. When he looked up by chance, he had the shock of his life: Lucie and her father! Lucie with her arms stretched out to him, and a look of intensity on her face that he had not seen for years.

"What is this?" cried Mr. Lorry, breathless and confused. "What is the matter? Lucie! Manette! What has happened? What has brought you here to Paris? What is it?"

With the look fixed upon him, in her paleness and wildness, she panted out in his arms, **imploringly**,[1] "O my dear friend! My husband!"

"Your husband, Lucie?"

"Charles."

"What of Charles?"

"Here."

"Here, in Paris?"

"Has been here some days—three or four—I don't know how many—I can't collect my thoughts. An errand of generosity brought him here unknown to us; he was stopped at the barrier and sent to prison."

The old man uttered a hoarse cry. Almost at the same moment, the bell of the great gate rang again, and a loud noise of feet and voices came pouring into the courtyard.

"What is that noise?" said the Doctor, turning towards the window.

---

[1] **imploringly**—begging urgently and piteously.

"Don't look!" cried Mr. Lorry. "Manette, for your life, don't touch the blinds!"

The Doctor turned, with his hand upon the fastening of the window, and said, with a calm, bold smile: "My dear friend, I have a charmed life in this city. I have been a Bastille prisoner. There is no patriot in Paris who, knowing me to have been a prisoner in the Bastille, would touch me, except to overwhelm me with embraces or carry me in triumph.[2] My old pain has given me a power that has brought us through the barrier, and gained us news of Charles. I knew it would be so; I knew I could help Charles out of danger; I told Lucie so. What is that noise?" His hand was again upon the window.

"Don't look!" cried Mr. Lorry, absolutely desperate. "No, Lucie, my dear, nor you! What prison is Charles in?"

"La Force."

"La Force! Lucie, my child, if ever you were brave and intelligent in your life—and you were always both—you will **compose**[3] yourself now, to do exactly as I tell you; for more depends upon it

---

[2] When the Bastille was overthrown by Defarge and others, the prisoners who were released were considered heroes. Dr. Manette, as a former prisoner, is also considered a hero. He hopes this special status will help him get Charles released from prison.

[3] **compose**—make (oneself) calm or tranquil.

than you can think, or I can say. You must leave your father and me alone for two minutes. Please, I beg you, do not delay!"

"I will obey you. I know I can trust you."

The old man hurried her into his room and turned the key. Then, he came hurrying back to the Doctor, opened the window, put his hand upon the Doctor's arm, and looked out with him into the courtyard at the throng of forty or fifty men and women. The throng had rushed in and set to work at a **grindstone**.[4]

But, such awful workers, and such awful work!

The grindstone had a double handle, and turning at it madly were two men whose long hair flapped back. When the whirling of the grindstone brought their faces up, they were shown to be more horrible and cruel than the faces of the wildest monsters. As they turned and turned, the women held wine to their mouths so that they might drink.

Shouldering one another to get to the sharpening stone were men stripped to the waist, with stains all over their limbs and bodies. Hatchets,

---

[4] **grindstone**—a revolving stone disk used for grinding, polishing, or sharpening tools. Now the mob's search for vengeance is totally out of control. Dickens set Darnay's return to Paris at the time of the September Massacres, when 1,089 prisoners were executed in four days.

knives, bayonets,[5] swords, were all brought to be sharpened.

All this the two men saw in a moment, and then they drew back from the window. The Doctor turned to his friend for an explanation.

"They are," Mr. Lorry whispered the words, glancing fearfully round at the locked room, "murdering the prisoners. If you are sure of what you say; if you really have the power you think you have, make yourself known to these devils, and have them take you to La Force. It may be too late, I don't know, but let it not be a minute later!"

Dr. Manette pressed his hand, and hastened from the room. For a moment he was out of sight, and then Mr. Lorry saw him, surrounded by a group of men and women. By listening closely, he could make out the calls of the crowd: "Long live the Bastille prisoner! Help the Bastille prisoner's family in La Force! Make room for the Bastille prisoner! Save the prisoner Evrémonde at La Force!" and a hundred answering shouts.

Mr. Lorry closed the window with a fluttering heart and hastened to Lucie, to tell her that her father was assisted by the people and had gone in

---

[5] bayonets—blades adapted to fit the muzzle end of a rifle and used as a weapon in close combat.

search of her husband. He found her child and Miss Pross with her, though he had failed to notice them before.

Miss Pross had laid the child down on his own bed. Lucie slept alongside her child. Gradually, even Miss Pross slept. But O, the long, long night, with the moans of the poor wife! And O, the long, long night, with no return of her father and no news!

Madame Defarge

Mr. Lorry knew that he must find a set of rooms to rent for Lucie. He knew he had no right to put the Bank in danger by sheltering the wife of an emigrant prisoner under the Bank roof. At first, his mind thought of Defarge and wondered if the wine shop owner would shelter the group. But then he thought again, and realized that Saint Antoine was now the most violent district in Paris.

Lucie told Mr. Lorry that her father had spoken of renting rooms for a short while in the district near Tellson's. So Mr. Lorry went out in search of such lodging, and found a suitable set of rooms on a quiet street full of deserted homes not too far from the Bank.

He moved Lucie, little Lucie, and Miss Pross to these rooms immediately. After they were settled, he returned to Tellson's to await news of Dr. Manette.

Later that evening, a man arrived at Tellson's and asked for Mr. Lorry by name.

"Good evening," said Mr. Lorry.

"Do you know me?" replied the man.

"I have seen you somewhere," Mr. Lorry said slowly.

He was a strong-looking man with dark curling hair, from forty-five to fifty years of age.

"Perhaps you've seen me at my wine shop?"

Much interested and agitated, Mr. Lorry said: "You come from Dr. Manette?"

"Yes. I come from Dr. Manette."

"And what does he say? What does he send me?"

Defarge handed over an open scrap of paper, on which were words in the Doctor's writing:

"Charles is safe, but I cannot safely leave this place yet. The bearer of this note has a short note from Charles to his wife. Let the bearer see his wife."

The note was dated from La Force, and was written within the past hour. "Will you come with me," said Mr. Lorry, in relieved tones, "to where his wife resides?"

"Yes," returned Defarge.

Scarcely noticing the reserved and mechanical way Defarge spoke, Mr. Lorry put on his hat and led the way down into the courtyard. There, they found two women; one of whom was knitting.

"Madame Defarge, surely!" said Mr. Lorry, who had left her in exactly the position some seventeen years ago.

"It is she," observed her husband.

"Does Madame go with us?" inquired Mr. Lorry, seeing that she moved as they moved.

"Yes. She needs to be able to recognize the faces and know the persons. It is for their safety."

Mr. Lorry looked curiously at Defarge, and then proceeded to lead the way. Both women followed, the second woman being The Vengeance.

They passed through the streets as quickly as they might, and arrived at Lucie's lodgings. They were admitted by Jerry, and found Lucie weeping, alone. She was overjoyed to hear Mr. Lorry's news, and clasped the hand that delivered this note:

"DEAREST,

Take courage. I am well, and your father has influence around me. You cannot answer this. Kiss our child for me."

That was all the writing. It was so much, however, to Lucie that she turned from Defarge to his wife, and kissed one of the hands that knitted. It was a passionate, loving, womanly action, but the hand made no response; instead, it dropped cold and heavy, and took to its knitting again.

There was something in the touch of Madame Defarge's hand that made Lucie pause. She gave Madame Defarge a frightened look. Madame Defarge returned Lucie's look with a cold, **impassive**[1] stare.

"My dear Lucie," said Mr. Lorry, in an attempt to explain, "there are frequent riots in the streets; and, although it is not likely they will ever trouble you, Madame Defarge wanted to see you so that she might protect you as needed."

"Is that his child?" said Madame Defarge, stopping in her work for the first time, and pointing her knitting needle at little Lucie.

---

[1] **impassive**—revealing no emotion; expressionless.

"Yes, Madame," answered Mr. Lorry; "this is Charles Darnay's darling daughter, and his only child."

The shadow from Madame Defarge and the other two seemed to fall so threatening and dark on the child that her mother instinctively kneeled on the ground beside her and held her to her breast.

The shadow seemed then to fall, threatening and dark, on both the mother and the child.

_____

"It is the daughter of your father who is my business here."

_____

"It is enough, my husband," said Madame Defarge. "I have seen them. We may go."

But something in Madame Defarge's tone of voice frightened Lucie enough to compel her to lay an appealing hand on Madame Defarge's dress and say: "You will be good to my poor husband. You will do him no harm. You will help me to see him if you can?"

"Your husband is not my business here," returned Madame Defarge, looking down at her with perfect composure. "It is the daughter of your father who is my business here."

"For my sake, then, be merciful to my husband. For my child's sake! We beg you to be merciful. We are more afraid of you than of these others."

Madame Defarge received this as a compliment, and looked at her husband, who had been uneasily biting his thumbnail. At her glance, he stood up straighter and assumed a stern expression.

"As a wife and mother," Lucie continued, "I implore you to have pity on me and my family. O sister-woman, think of me as a wife and mother!"

Madame Defarge looked, coldly as ever, at Lucie and said, turning to The Vengeance, "The wives and mothers we have known, since we were as little as this child, have never been pitied. Their husbands and fathers have laid in prison for years. All our lives, we have seen our sister-women suffer from poverty, nakedness, hunger, thirst, sickness, and despair."

"We have seen nothing else," added The Vengeance.

"We have endured this a long time," said Madame Defarge, turning her eyes again upon Lucie. "You decide. Do you think that the trouble of one wife and mother would mean much to us now?"

She picked up her knitting and left without another word. The Vengeance followed. Defarge went last, and closed the door.

La Force

Dr. Manette did not return until the morning of the fourth day of his absence. During the time that he was away, eleven hundred defenseless prisoners of both sexes and all ages had been killed by the people. Those four days and nights had been darkened by this deed of horror.

When they were alone, Dr. Manette told his story to Mr. Lorry. The crowd from the grindstone had taken him through a scene of **carnage**[1] to the prison of La Force. In the prison, he had come upon a self-appointed Tribunal before which the prisoners were brought one at a time. The Tribunal decided

---

[1] **carnage**—massive slaughter.

whether the prisoner should be released or executed. In most cases, they were executed.

Dr. Manette presented himself to the Tribunal, announced his name and profession and that he had been a secret and unaccused prisoner in the Bastille. Defarge, who sat on the Tribunal, had identified him. Dr. Manette explained that his son-in-law was there at La Force. He had come to ask for the man's life and liberty.

Dr. Manette felt now, for the first time, that his suffering for the long eighteen years could actually become a source of strength and power for him.

The Tribunal conferred in private and then announced that the emigrant Evrémonde would be spared. He would remain in prison, but he would be unharmed. With that promise, Dr. Manette returned to his daughter.

Because of his experiences at La Force, Dr. Manette felt now, for the first time, that his suffering for the long eighteen years could actually become a source of strength and power for him. His years in prison had given him the power to break down the prison door of his daughter's husband, and deliver him. "My life, you see," he explained, "is not mere waste and ruin. As my beloved child was helpful in restoring me to myself, I will be helpful now in restoring the dearest part of herself to her; by the aid of heaven I will do it!"

Over the course of the next day, the Doctor was able to achieve another triumph. He convinced the Republic to allow him to become the inspecting physician of three prisons, including La Force. He told Lucie that he would see her husband weekly, and that he would keep a careful watch on him.

So the time passed. One day, when Charles had been in prison for one year and three months, the Doctor told Lucie that Charles would be summoned before the Tribunal the next day.

The dread Tribunal of five judges, a prosecutor, and a determined jury sat every day. Their lists went forth every evening, and were read out by the gaolers of the various prisons to their prisoners. The standard gaoler joke was, "Come out and listen to the Evening Paper, you inside there!"

"Charles Evrémonde, called Darnay!" So at last began the Evening Paper at La Force.

When a name was called, its owner stepped apart into a spot reserved for those who were announced. His gaoler, who wore spectacles to read with, glanced over them to assure himself that he had taken his place, and then went through the list, making a similar short pause at each name. There were twenty-three names, but only twenty were responded to; for one of the prisoners so summoned had died in jail and been forgotten, and two had already been guillotined and forgotten.

On the day of the Tribunal, fifteen prisoners appeared before the judge before Charles Darnay's name was called. All the fifteen were condemned to death.

When it was his turn, he heard his name— "Charles Evrémonde, called Darnay"—and went without hesitating to stand before the group.

Looking at the jury and the noisy audience, Darnay might have thought that the usual order of things was reversed, and that the **felons**[2] were trying the honest men. The lowest, cruelest, and worst people of the city sat in judgment of the prisoners before them. The men were all armed in various ways; of the women, some wore knives, some daggers, some ate and drank as they looked

---

[2] **felons**—criminals.

on, many knitted. Among these last was Madame Defarge, whom Charles had not met, but had heard about.

In nearby chairs sat Dr. Manette and Mr. Lorry. As well as the prisoner could see, he and Mr. Lorry were the only men there who were unconnected with the Tribunal.

Charles Evrémonde, called Darnay, was accused by the public prosecutor as an emigrant. As such, his life must be **forfeited**[3] to the Republic.

"Take off his head!" cried the audience. "An enemy to the Republic!"

The President rang his bell to silence those cries, and asked the prisoner whether it was not true that he had lived many years in England.

Undoubtedly it was.

Was he not an emigrant then? What did he call himself?

Not an emigrant, he hoped, within the sense and spirit of the law.

Why not? the President desired to know.

Because he had voluntarily relinquished a title that was distasteful to him, and a station that was

---

[3] **forfeited**—given up.

distasteful to him, and had left France to live by his own industry in England, rather than on the industry of the overworked people of France.

What proof had he of this?

He handed in the names of two witnesses: Théophile Gabelle and Alexandre Manette.

But he had married in England, the President reminded him.

True, but not an English woman.

A citizeness of France?

Yes. By birth.

Her name and family?

"Lucie Manette, only daughter of Dr. Manette, the good physician who sits there."

This answer had a happy effect upon the audience. Cries of welcome to Dr. Manette rang out in the hall.

The President then asked why had he returned to France when he did and not sooner?

He had not returned sooner, he replied, simply because he had no means of living in France. In England, he lived by giving instruction in the French language and literature. He had returned when he did, on the pressing and written entreaty of a French citizen, who said that his life was endangered by his absence. He had come back to save a citizen's life. Did that make him a criminal in the eyes of the Republic?

The populace cried enthusiastically, "No!"

Citizen Gabelle was called to confirm the story, and did so. Citizen Gabelle hinted, with great politeness, that in the pressure of business imposed on the Tribunal, he had been slightly overlooked in his prison until three days ago. Dr. Manette was questioned next. His honest, steady manner made a great impression on the room.

After Dr. Manette testified, the Tribunal took its vote. At every vote (the jurymen voted aloud and individually), the people sent up a shout of applause. All the voices were in the prisoner's favor and the President declared him free.

> **Once they had carried him outside, they hoisted him above their heads and called out for all to see, "He is free! The prisoner of the Republic is free!"**

In a wild, exuberant show of support, the crowd swooped around Charles and carried him out of the hall. Tears were shed as freely as blood another time. Once they had carried him outside, they hoisted him above their heads and called out for all to see, "He is free! The prisoner of the Republic is free!" On they carried him, through the streets and avenues of the district. Then, with one final burst of frenzied excitement, they carried him into the courtyard of the building where his wife lived. When her husband stood on his feet, a nearly speechless Lucie ran out the door and dropped unconscious into his arms.

As he held her to his heart and looked upon her beautiful face, a few of the people fell to dancing. Instantly, all the rest fell to dancing, and the courtyard overflowed with **revelers**.[4]

After grasping the Doctor's hand, who stood victorious and proud before him; after grasping the hand of Mr. Lorry, who came panting in breathless from his struggle against the crowd; after kissing little Lucie, who was lifted up to clasp her arms round his neck; and after embracing the devoted and faithful Pross who lifted her; Charles took his wife in his arms, and carried her up to their apartment.

"Lucie! My own! I am safe."

"O dearest Charles, thank God!"

"And thank your father, dearest. No other man in all of France could have done what he has done for me."

---

[4] **revelers**—merrymakers.

She laid her head upon her father's breast, as she had laid his poor head on her own breast, long, long ago. He, who was proud of his newfound strength, said: "You must not be weak, my darling. Don't tremble so. I have saved him."[5]

---

[5] At long last, Dr. Manette can say that his horrible imprisonment served a purpose, since it allowed him to help Darnay. Compare this picture of Dr. Manette, newly courageous, to the trembling, confused man of Book One.

A Knock at the Door

"I have saved him." It was not a dream. He was really here. And yet his wife trembled, for she could not relax. Her fear for his safety stayed upon her.

Drained and exhausted, Charles sat near to the fire in his wife's rocker. She sat by his side, unwilling to let go of him even for a moment.

For the months that Charles had been imprisoned, Miss Pross and Jerry Cruncher together had done the shopping for the household. The afternoon that Charles Darnay was released, the two ventured out together to shop for a celebration meal.

"Now, Mr. Cruncher," said Miss Pross, whose eyes were red with happiness, "if you are ready, I am."

Jerry hoarsely professed himself at Miss Pross's service.

"There's all manner of things wanted," said Pross. "Now, Ladybird, never you stir from that fire till I come back! Take care of the dear husband you have recovered, and don't move your pretty head from his shoulder till you see me again! May I ask a question, Dr. Manette, before I go?"

"I think you may take that liberty," the Doctor answered, smiling.

> **"But here is my question: is there any prospect of our getting out of this place?"**

"For gracious sake, don't talk about Liberty; we have had quite enough of that," said Miss Pross. "But here is my question: is there any prospect of our getting out of this place?"

"I fear not yet. It would be dangerous for Charles."

"Heigh-ho-hum!" said Miss Pross, cheerfully repressing a sigh as she glanced at her darling Ladybird, "then we must have patience and wait. We must hold up our heads and fight low, as my brother Solomon used to say. Now, Mr. Cruncher, we're off!"

They went out, leaving Lucie, her husband, her father, and the child by a bright fire. Little Lucie sat by her grandfather with her hands clasped through his arm: and he, in a tone not rising much above a whisper, began to tell her a story of a great and powerful fairy who had opened a prison wall and let out a captive who had once done the fairy a service. All was subdued and quiet, and Lucie was just a bit more at ease.

"What is that?" she cried, all at once.

"My dear!" said her father, stopping in his story, and laying his hand on hers, "control yourself. What a state you are in! The least thing—nothing—startles you! You, your father's daughter!"

"I thought, my father," said Lucie, excusing herself, with a pale face and in a faltering voice, "that I heard strange feet upon the stairs."

"My love, the staircase is as still as death." As he said the word, a blow was struck upon the door.

"Oh Father, Father! What can this be! Hide Charles. Save him!"

"My child," said the Doctor, rising and laying his hand upon her shoulder, "I *have* saved him. What weakness is this, my dear! Let me go to the door."

He took the lamp in his hand, crossed the room, and opened the door. Four rough men in red caps, armed with **sabers**[1] and pistols, entered the room.

> "Tell me how and why am I again a prisoner?"

"The Citizen Evrémonde, called Darnay," said the first.

"Who seeks him?" answered Darnay.

"I seek him. We seek him. I know you, Evrémonde; I saw you before the Tribunal today. You are once again the prisoner of the Republic."

The four surrounded him, where he stood with his wife and child clinging to him.

"Tell me how and why am I again a prisoner?"

"You will know tomorrow. For now, you must come."

With these words, Manette confronted the speaker, saying: "You know him, you have said. Do you know me?"

"Yes, I know you, Citizen Doctor."

"We all know you, Citizen Doctor," said the other three.

---

[1] **sabers**—swords with a curved edge.

The Doctor looked from one to another, and said, in a lower voice, after a pause: "Will you answer his question to me then? What is happening here?"

"Citizen Doctor," said the first, reluctantly, "he has been accused by Saint Antoine."

"Of what?" asked the Doctor.

"Citizen Doctor," said the first, "ask no more. If the Republic demands sacrifices from you, without a doubt, you as a good patriot will be happy to make them. Evrémonde, we are pressed for time."

"One word," the Doctor entreated. "Will you tell me who **denounced**[2] him?"

"It is against the rules," answered the first. "Truly it is against the rules. But he is denounced by the Citizen and Citizeness Defarge. And by one other."

"What other?"

Replied the man, with a strange look, "You will be answered tomorrow. Now, I am silent!"

---

[2] **denounced**—accused publicly.

Solomon

Happily unconscious of the new **calamity**[1] at home, Miss Pross threaded her way along the narrow streets and crossed the river by the bridge of the Pont-Neuf.[2] Mr. Cruncher, with the basket, walked at her side. They both looked to the right and to the left into most of the shops they passed. It was a damp and chilly evening, so they walked briskly.

After she purchased a few small articles of grocery and some oil for the lamp, Miss Pross remembered the wine they wanted. After peeping into several wine shops, she stopped at the sign of The Good Republican Brutus of Antiquity. It

---

[1] **calamity**—disaster.
[2] Pont-Neuf—a bridge on the northern side of Paris.

had a quieter look than any other wine shop, so Miss Pross decided to buy the wine here.

The two customers approached the counter, and showed what they wanted. As their wine was measured out, a man parted from another man in the corner, and rose to depart. In going, he had to face Miss Pross. No sooner did he face her, than Miss Pross uttered a scream and clapped her hands to her face.

No sooner did he face her, than Miss Pross uttered a scream and clapped her hands to her face.

In a moment, everyone in the shop was on their feet. Everybody looked to see if someone was bleeding, but only saw a man and a woman standing staring at each other. The man had the look of a Frenchman; the woman was evidently English.

"What is the matter?" said the man who had caused Miss Pross to scream, speaking in an angry, abrupt voice.

"Oh, Solomon, dear Solomon!" cried Miss Pross, clapping her hands again. "After not setting eyes upon you or hearing of you for so long a time, I find you here!"

"Don't call me Solomon. Do you want to be the death of me?" asked the man, in a **furtive**,[3] frightened way.

---

[3] **furtive**—secretive.

"Oh, brother, brother!" cried Miss Pross, and ran out of the shop. Her brother and Mr. Cruncher followed.

"Now," said Solomon, stopping at the dark street corner, "what do you want?"

"How dreadfully unkind in a brother," cried Miss Pross, "to give me such a greeting, and show me no affection."

"There. Darn it! There," said Solomon, making a dab at Miss Pross's lips with his own. "Now are you content?"

Miss Pross only shook her head and wept in silence.

"If you expect me to be surprised," said her brother Solomon, "I am not surprised; I knew you were here; I know of most people who are here. If you really don't want to endanger my existence—which I half believe you do—go your way as soon as possible, and let me go mine. I am busy. I am an official."

"My brother Solomon," mourned Miss Pross, casting up her tear-fraught eyes. "You who had the makings to be one of the best and greatest men in England, an official among foreigners, and such foreigners!"

Good Miss Pross! As if the separation between them was any fault of hers. Mr. Lorry had known it for a fact that years ago this precious brother had spent Miss Pross's money and left her destitute.

Mr. Cruncher, touching him on the shoulder, hoarsely interrupted with the following question: "I say! Is your name John Solomon, or Solomon John?"

The brother turned towards him with sudden distrust.

"Come!" said Mr. Cruncher. "Speak up! Is it John Solomon or Solomon John? She calls you Solomon, and she must know, being your sister. And I know you as John."

"What do you mean?"

"I know you. You was a spy-witness at the Bailey. You were called—you were called—"

"John Barsad, I believe," struck in Sydney Carton, who, with his hands behind his riding coat, stood at Mr. Cruncher's elbow as easily as he might have stood at the Old Bailey itself.

Miss Pross and Jerry Cruncher both jumped at the sound of his voice.

Mr. Carton offered a small smile. "Don't be alarmed, my dear Miss Pross. I arrived at Mr. Lorry's, to his surprise, yesterday evening; we agreed that I would not present myself elsewhere until all was well, or unless I could be useful; I present myself here, to beg a little talk with your brother. I wish for your sake Mr. Barsad was not a **sheep**[4] of the prisons."

After a pause, he continued. "I saw you, Mr. Barsad, coming out of the prison an hour or more ago. You have a face to be remembered, and I remember faces well."

"What do you want with me?" the spy asked, with some anger.

"It would be dangerous to explain in the street. Please follow me, as you'll be most interested in what I have to say," answered Mr. Carton. "But first we must conduct your sister safely to the corner of her own street, and as her escort knows Mr. Barsad, I will invite him to Mr. Lorry's with us."

Miss Pross recalled soon afterwards, and to the end of her life, that as she pressed her hands on Sydney's arm and looked up in his face, begging him to do no harm to Solomon, there was a strength and kindness in his eyes, which somehow changed and raised the man.

They left her at the corner of the street, and Carton led the way to Mr. Lorry's, which was but a minute or two away. John Barsad, or Solomon Pross, walked at his side.

---

[4] **sheep**—sheep was the name given to a spy for the jailers.

A Game of Cards

Mr. Lorry had just finished his dinner and was sitting before a cheery fire when the three men arrived. He turned his head as they entered, and showed his surprise.

"Miss Pross's brother, sir," said Carton. "Mr. Barsad."

"Barsad?" repeated the old gentleman, "Barsad? I recall the name and face."

"I told you you had a remarkable face, Mr. Barsad," observed Carton, coolly. "Pray sit down."

As he took a chair himself, he supplied the link that Mr. Lorry wanted by saying, "He was a witness at the Darnay trial, Mr. Lorry."

Lorry immediately remembered, and regarded his new visitor with disgust.

"It turns out that Mr. Barsad is also the affectionate brother you've heard Miss Pross speak of, by the name of Solomon," said Carton. "Now I pass to worse news. Darnay has been arrested again."

Struck with consternation, the old gentleman exclaimed, "But he's been out and free for just two hours!"

Carton did not reply. Instead, he said with a thoughtful air: "Now, I trust that the name and influence of Dr. Manette may stand him in good stead tomorrow. But it may not be so. I must admit, I am shaken, Mr. Lorry, by Dr. Manette's not having had the power to prevent this arrest."

"He may not have known of it beforehand," said Mr. Lorry.

"But that seems even more alarming, if you recall how identified he is with his son-in-law."

"That's true," Mr. Lorry acknowledged, with his troubled eyes on Carton.

"In short," said Carton, "this is a desperate time, when desperate games are played for desperate **stakes**.[1] Let the Doctor play the winning game; I will play the losing one. A man's life is

---

[1] **stakes**—wagers in a game, race, or contest.

worth very little here, in the new France. Now, the stake I have resolved to play for, in case of the worst, is a friend in the Republic. And the friend I set myself to win is Mr. Barsad."

"You'll need to have very good cards, sir," said the spy, rather smugly.

"I'll look them over, and see what I hold. Mr. Lorry, you know what a brute I am; I wish you'd give me a little brandy."

It was put before him, and he drank off a glassful and then pushed the bottle away.

"Mr. Barsad," he said, in the tone of one who really was looking at a hand at cards. "You are an Englishman; you are a spy for the British, yet you say you support the New French Republic. You have been a prisoner in England, yet you are a turnkey working at a French prison. You have a false name, you are a spy, a secret informer, yet you worked for the aristocrat English government, the enemy to France and Freedom. Those are excellent cards I'm holding. In fact, they are cards not to be beaten. Have you followed my hand, Mr. Barsad?"

"I understand your play," returned the spy, uneasily.

"If I play my ace, I will give up Mr. Barsad to the nearest Section Committee. Look over your hand, Mr. Barsad, and see what you have. Don't hurry." He drew the bottle near, poured out another glassful of brandy, and drank it off. "Look over your hand carefully, Mr. Barsad. Take your time."

In fact, it was a poorer hand than Sydney Carton suspected. Barsad knew that he had accepted work in France, first as a tempter of his own countrymen, then, gradually, as a tempter among the natives. Under the overthrown government, he had spied upon Saint Antoine and Defarge's wine shop. Barsad always remembered with fear and trembling that that terrible Defarge woman had knitted when he talked with her, and had looked ominously at him as her fingers moved. He had since seen her, in the district of Saint Antoine, over and over again produce her knitted registers and denounce people whose lives the guillotine then surely swallowed up. He knew in his heart that that dreadful woman had knitted his name into her register.

> **"All right, sir. I admit that I am a spy, and that it is considered a disgraceful job."**

"You scarcely seem to like your hand," said Carton. "Do you intend to play?"

"All right, sir. I admit that I am a spy, and that it is considered a disgraceful job."

"I play my ace, Mr. Barsad," said Carton, taking the answer on himself, and looking at his watch, "without any hesitation in a very few minutes."

"I should have hoped, gentlemen," said the spy, trying to hook Mr. Lorry into the discussion, "that your respect for my sister—"

"I could not better show my respect for your sister than by finally relieving her of her brother," said Sydney Carton. "And indeed, now that I think about it, I have a strong impression that I have another good card here, not yet played. Your friend in the wine shop. Who was he?"

"French. You don't know him," said the spy quickly.

"Hmmm. And yet I know the face."

"I think not. I am sure not. It can't be," said the spy.

"It—can't—be," muttered Sydney Carton, thoughtfully. "No. English!" cried Carton, striking his open hand on the table, as a light broke clearly on his mind. "Cly! It is Cly. We heard from him at Darnay's trial at the Old Bailey."

"Now, there you are mistaken, sir," said Barsad, with a smile. "Cly has been dead several years. He was buried in London. Here is a certificate of his burial, which I happen to have with me." Barsad laid the document before Mr. Carton and Mr. Lorry.

As the two men studied the document, Mr. Cruncher—who had been silent for some time now—turned to Barsad, and said: "That there Roger Cly, master. So you put him in his coffin?"

"I did."

"Who took him out of it?"

Barsad leaned back in his chair and stammered, "What do you mean?"

"I mean," said Mr. Cruncher, "that he wasn't never in it. No! Not he!"

The spy looked at Carton and Lorry; they both looked in astonishment at Jerry.

"I tell you," said Jerry, "that you buried paving stones and earth in that there coffin. Don't go and tell me that you buried Cly. It was a trick. Me and two more knows it."

"How do you know it?"

"What's that to you? Egod!" growled Mr. Cruncher, "it's you I have got an old grudge against, it is, with your shameful tricks upon honest tradesmen such as myself!"

Sydney Carton, who, with Mr. Lorry, had been silent with amazement, asked Mr. Cruncher to explain himself.

"At another time, sir," he replied, mysteriously, "the present time is ill-convenient for explainin'.

What you need to know, sirs, is that Cly was never in that there coffin."

"So, Mr. Barsad! Yet another card. You are a spy, and you are in league with still another spy—Mr. Cly, who faked his own death. That is a strong card—a guillotine card! Will you play?"

"No!" returned the spy. "I give up. I confess that we were so unpopular with the mob that I barely got away from England. Cly would never have got away at all if it weren't for that **sham**[2] burial. Though how this man knows it was a sham is a wonder of wonders to me.

"But your game, Mr. Carton, must come to a point. I go on duty soon and can't be late. Now what do you want with me?"

Carton began: "You are a turnkey at the Conciergerie?"[3]

"I am sometimes."

"You can be when you choose."

"I can pass in and out when I choose."

"So far, we have spoken before these two, because they too must understand our game of cards," said Carton. "But now the game will change. Come into the front room here, and let us have one final word alone."

---

[2] **sham**—fake.
[3] Conciergerie—prison in the Justice Palace.

The Game Is Made

While Sydney Carton and Barsad were in the next room, speaking so low that not a sound was heard, Mr. Lorry looked at Jerry in considerable doubt and mistrust.

"Jerry," said Mr. Lorry. "Come here."

Mr. Cruncher came forward sideways, with one shoulder ahead of the other.

"What have you been, besides a messenger?"

After some thought, Mr. Cruncher replied, "I've been sort of an agricultural man."

"I am concerned," said Mr. Lorry, angrily shaking a forefinger at him, "that you have used the respectable and great house of Tellson's as a blind, and that you have all along been working as a resurrection-man. If you have, don't expect me to befriend you when you get back to England. Don't expect me to keep your secret."

"I hope, sir," pleaded the **abashed**[1] Mr. Cruncher, "that a gentleman like yourself wot I've had the honor of odd-jobbing till I'm gray at it, would think twice about harming me, even if it was true. Remember wot I said just now to that rascal about Cly, and how that will be helping our dear friends, especially Mr. Darnay."

"That at least is true," said Mr. Lorry. "Say no more now. It may be that I shall yet stand as your friend, if you deserve it."

In another moment, Sydney Carton and the spy returned from the dark room. "Adieu, Mr. Barsad," said Carton. "Our arrangements thus made, you have nothing to fear from me."

Carton sat down in a chair near the fireplace beside Mr. Lorry. When they were alone, Mr. Lorry asked him what he had done.

"Not much. If it should go badly at the prison, I will be able to see him, once."

Mr. Lorry's face fell.

"It is all I could do," said Carton. "To propose too much would be to put this man's head under the ax, which will do none of us a bit of good."

---

[1] **abashed**—ashamed and uneasy.

"But seeing Darnay," said Mr. Lorry, "will not save him."

"I never said it would."

Mr. Lorry stared at the fire. His sympathy for his darling, and the heavy disappointment of this second arrest, had gradually weakened him; he was an old man now, and his tears fell.

"You are a good man and a true friend," said Carton gently. "Please try not to worry. And please don't tell Lucie of this interview, or this arrangement. In fact, don't speak of me at all. It's best that she not know I am here. It would only add to her troubles. You are going to her, I hope? She must be very lonely tonight."

"I am going now, directly."

"I am glad of that. She has such a strong attachment to you and reliance on you. How does she look?"

"Anxious and unhappy, but very beautiful."

"Ah, yes!" It was a long, grieving sound, like a sigh—almost like a sob. "She is so beautiful."

After another moment, Carton asked, "Have your duties at Tellson's Paris Bank drawn to an end, sir?"

"Yes. I am ready to leave for London."

"You have been useful all your life, Mr. Lorry; you have been steadily and constantly occupied; trusted, respected, and looked up to," said Mr. Carton wistfully.

"I have been a man of business ever since I have been a man, and I am in my seventy-eighth year. Indeed, I may say that I was a man of business when a boy."

"Indeed, I may say that I was a man of business when a boy."

"What a place you fill! So many people will miss you when you leave it empty!"

"A solitary old bachelor," answered Mr. Lorry, shaking his head. "There is nobody to weep for me."

"How can you say that? Wouldn't Lucie weep for you? Wouldn't her child?"

"Yes, yes, thank God. I didn't quite mean what I said."

"It is a thing to thank God for; is it not?"

"Surely, surely. But you, Mr. Carton, are so young. You have your whole life."

"Yes," said Carton sadly. "I am not old, but I have not been young for years and years, it seems. But enough of me."

"And of me, I am sure," said Mr. Lorry. "Are you going out?"

"Yes. You know my restless habits. If I should prowl about the streets a long time, don't be uneasy; I shall reappear in the morning. You'll go to the court tomorrow to see Darnay's fate?"

"Yes, unhappily."

"I shall be there, as well, but only as one of the crowd. My spy will find a place for me. Take my arm, sir."

Mr. Lorry did so, and they went downstairs and out in the streets.

Carton had not gone far out of sight when he stopped in the middle of the street under a glimmering lamp and wrote with his pencil on a scrap of paper. Then, traveling with the step of one who knew the streets well, he made his way to a **chemist's shop**[2] and handed his scrap to the man at the counter.

"Whew!" the chemist whistled softly, as he read it. "For you, citizen?"

"For me."

"You will be careful to keep them separate, citizen? You know the consequences of mixing them?"

"Perfectly."

Certain small packets were made and given to him. He put them, one by one, in the breast pocket

---

[2] **chemist's shop**—drugstore.

of his inner coat, counted out the money for them, and left the shop. "There is nothing more to do," said he, glancing upward at the moon, "until tomorrow. I can't sleep, so I will walk."

Long ago, when he had been famous among his competitors as a youth of great promise, he had had the sad responsibility of watching his father be buried. These solemn words, which had been read at his father's grave, arose in his mind as he went down the dark streets, among the heavy shadows, with the moon high above him. *"I am the resurrection and the life, saith the Lord: he that believeth in me, though he were dead, yet shall he live: and whosoever liveth and believeth in me, shall never die."* As he walked, he repeated these words to himself. *"I am the resurrection and the life, saith the Lord. . . ."*

The streets were quiet tonight. The words were in the echoes of his feet, and were in the air. Perfectly calm and steady, he said them to himself as he walked. Even when his thoughts turned elsewhere, he heard the words in the back of his mind.

At last, the night wore itself out. The glorious sun, rising, seemed to strike at the words he had repeated all night, and his heart grew lighter and warmer, and a bridge of light seemed to span the air between him and the sun, while the river ran under it. The river seemed like an old friend. He walked away from the houses and in the light and warmth of the sun fell asleep on the bank. When he woke, he watched a ripple in the water that turned and turned and then was absorbed by the stream and carried out to the sea. "Like me!" The prayer took on new meaning for him: "I am the resurrection and the life," he whispered. Then he turned his feet in the direction of the court.[3]

The court was all astir and abuzz by the time Carton arrived. Mr. Lorry was there, as was Dr. Manette. And Lucie was there, sitting beside her father.

When her husband was brought in, she turned a look upon him, so sustaining, so encouraging, so full of admiring love and tenderness that it helped Darnay to stand a bit straighter and hold his head higher. Sydney Carton watched all this and felt his heart grow warm.

After Darnay took his seat, every eye turned to the jury. The same determined patriots and good republicans as yesterday and the day before, and

---

[3] Carton's soul searching during the night has left him with a new sense of purpose. He understands now that he has the strength to help those he loves. The Sydney Carton who turns his feet in the direction of the court is a stronger, more courageous man.

tomorrow, and the day after, were all there. Eager and prominent among them was Defarge and Jacques Three of Saint Antoine.

Without wasting a moment, the President asked: who denounced the accused?

The response: "Three people. The first: Ernest Defarge, wine vendor of Saint Antoine."

"Good."

"The second: Thérèse Defarge, his wife."

"Good."

"And the third: Alexandre Manette, physician."

A great uproar took place in the court, and in the midst of it, Dr. Manette was seen, pale and trembling, standing where he had been seated.

"President, I indignantly protest to you that this is a fraud. You know the accused to be the husband of my daughter. My daughter, and those dear to her, are far dearer to me than my life. I have accused this man of nothing!"

"Citizen Manette, be still. Listen to what is to follow. In the meanwhile, be silent!"

D_{r.} Manette sat down, with his eyes looking around, and his lips trembling. He listened as Defarge told the story of the Doctor's imprisonment.

A short examination followed, for the court was quick with its work.

"You were present at the taking of the Bastille, citizen?"

"Yes."

"Inform the Tribunal of what you did that day within the Bastille, citizen."

"I knew," said Defarge, looking down at his wife, "I knew that Dr. Manette had been confined in a cell known as One Hundred and Five, North Tower. I knew it from himself. I went to examine his cell. In a hole in the chimney, where a stone had been worked out and replaced, I found a paper, written in his hand."

"Let it be read."

In a dead silence and stillness, Defarge took the paper, cleared his throat, and then began to read.

The Substance
of the Shadow

"I, Alexandre Manette, physician, native of
Beauvais, and afterwards resident of Paris, write
this sad paper in my cell in the Bastille during
the last month of the year 1767. I write it at stolen
intervals, under every difficulty. I will hide it in the
wall of the chimney in the hopes that some pitying
hand may find it there when I and my sorrows
are dust.

"My story is this. One cloudy, moonlit night, in
the third week of December, in the year 1757, I was
walking by the **Seine**[1] when a carriage came along

---

[1] **Seine**—river that flows through the heart of Paris.

behind me, driven very fast. As I stood aside to let the carriage pass, a head was put out at the window, and a voice called to the driver to stop.

"The carriage stopped as soon as the driver could rein in his horses, and the same voice called to me by my name. I answered. Two men, who were both wrapped in cloaks and appeared to conceal themselves, stepped out. As they stood at the carriage door, I observed that they both looked of about my own age, or rather younger, and that they were greatly alike, in stature, manner, voice, and (as far as I could see) face, too.

"'You are Dr. Manette?' said one.

"'I am.'

"'We have been looking for you. Will you please to enter the carriage?'

"'Gentlemen,' said I, 'pardon me; but I must know why you need me.'

"'Doctor, you'll understand soon enough. Will you please to enter the carriage?'

"As they were armed, I could do nothing but go along. The carriage turned about, and drove away at a great speed.

"We soon left the city behind, and traveled a distance on a country road. Presently we stopped at a solitary house. We all three made our way to the door of the house. By the light I saw that my companions were twin brothers.

"As we entered the house, I heard cries coming from an upstairs room. The brothers led me upstairs and showed me into a small room. There I found a patient in a high fever of the brain, lying on a bed.

"The patient was a woman of great beauty, and young; probably not much past twenty. Her hair was torn and ragged, and her arms were bound to her sides with scarves and handkerchiefs. On one of them, a fringed scarf, I saw the crest of a nobleman, and the letter *E*. In her restlessness she had turned over on her face on the edge of the bed.

"I approached the patient, turned her over gently, and looked into her face. Her eyes were dilated and wild, and she constantly uttered piercing shrieks and repeated the words, 'My husband, my father, and my brother!' and then counted up to twelve, and said, 'Hush!' For an instant, and no more, she would pause to listen, and then the piercing shrieks would begin again, and she would repeat the cry, 'My husband, my father, and my brother!' and would count up to twelve, and say 'Hush!'

"'How long,' I asked, 'has this lasted?'

"The brother that I took to be older, for he seemed to have more authority, replied, 'Since about this hour last night.'

"I gave the woman a **narcotic**[2] to calm her. There was little else to do. I sat by the side of the bed for half an hour, with the two brothers looking on, before the elder brother said: 'There is another patient.'

"I was startled and asked, 'Is it a pressing case?'

"'You had better see,' he carelessly answered and led me across the hall to another room.

"The other patient lay in a back room across a second staircase. On some hay on the floor, with a cushion thrown under his head, lay a handsome peasant boy of not more than seventeen. I saw immediately that he was dying of a sword wound to his chest.

"'How has this been done, monsieur?' said I to the elder brother.

"'He is a crazed young **serf**![3] He forced my brother to draw upon him, and has fallen by my brother's sword.' There was no touch of pity or sorrow in the man's voice.

---

[2] **narcotic**—drug that affects the mind, inducing stupor or sleep.

[3] **serf**—member of a servant class of people in Europe who were bound to the land and owned by a lord. A serf could not be sold off the land. Instead, he or she was passed from owner to owner.

"The boy's eyes had slowly moved to him as he had spoken, and they now slowly moved to me. 'Doctor, they are very proud, these nobles; but we common serfs are proud too. They steal from us, beat us, and kill us; but we have a little pride left, sometimes. She—have you seen her, Doctor?'

"I said, 'I have seen her.'

"'She is my sister, Doctor. She was a good girl. She was **betrothed**[4] to a good man, too: a **tenant**[5] of the Marquis, who stands there. The other is his brother, the worst of a bad race. We have been taxed by these men without mercy, made to work for them without pay, and have lived lives of misery at their hands.'

"'Nevertheless, Doctor, my sister married. She had not been married many weeks when the Marquis's brother asked her husband to lend her to him. He was willing enough, but my sister was good and virtuous and hated his brother with a hatred as strong as mine.'

"'To force her to change her mind, these two nobles harnessed the husband to a cart and drove

---

[4] **betrothed**—engaged to be married.
[5] **tenant**—person who rents land or property from a landlord.

him to exhaustion. On his last day, he made his way to my sister, sobbed twelve times, once for every stroke of the bell, and died on her bosom.'

"'Then, the Marquis's brother took my sister for his pleasure for a little while. I tracked him here and last night climbed in the house and attacked him. He drew his sword to defend himself and wounded me thus.'

"Next, the wounded boy raised up. 'Marquis,' he said, 'in the days when all these things are to be answered for, I summon you and yours, to the last of your bad race, to answer for them. I mark this cross of blood upon you, as a sign that I will do it. I summon your brother, the worst of the bad race, to answer for them separately.'

"Twice, the boy put his hand to the wound in his breast, and with a forefinger drew a cross in the air. He left his finger in the air for another moment, and then as his hand dropped, he dropped with it, and I laid him down dead.

"When I returned to the bedside of the woman, I found her close to death. Still she cried, 'My husband, my father, and my brother! One, two, three, four, five, six, seven, eight, nine, ten, eleven, twelve. Hush!' This lasted twenty-six hours, and then she died.

"I told the Marquis that she had died. He said, 'At last!' And then he made a request: 'Doctor, I ask that the things that you have seen here are things to be seen and not spoken of.'

"When both brothers understood that the woman was dead, they offered me money, which I declined. I then returned home.

"Early the next morning, I found a bag of gold in a little box outside my door. I decided that day to write privately to the Minister, stating the nature of the two cases to which I had been summoned, and the place to which I had gone. I knew what Court influence was, and what the **immunities**[6] of the nobles were, and I expected that the matter would never be heard of; but I wished to relieve my own mind. I had kept the matter a profound secret even from my wife; and this, too, I resolved to state in my letter.

"Of course, I had no knowledge of my real danger.

"Just as I was finishing my letter, I was told that a lady waited, who wished to see me. The lady told me she was the wife of the Marquis St. Evrémonde—the elder of the two brothers I had met was her husband. She knew the whole cruel story, and her husband's part in it. She then pointed

---

[6] **immunities**—protection from laws; exemptions.

to the two- or three-year-old child who was with her, and said:

"'This child must do what he can to make amends for the horrors caused by the Evrémonde family.' Then she kissed the boy and said, caressing him, 'It is for your own dear sake. You will be faithful, little Charles?' The child answered her bravely, 'Yes!' I kissed her hand, and she took him in her arms, and went away. I never saw her again.

"After she left, I sealed my letter and delivered it myself. That night, a man in a black coat rang at my gate, demanded to see me, and softly followed my servant, Ernest Defarge, a youth, upstairs. When they came into the room where I sat with my wife—my wife, beloved of my heart!—the man said to me, 'An urgent case in the Rue St. Honoré.' He told me that he had a coach waiting.

"My wife begged me not to go, but I told her not to worry. Of course she was right—she seemed to know the danger, even if I did not.

"When I was clear of the house, a black scarf was drawn tightly over my mouth from behind, and my arms were tied. The two brothers crossed the road from a dark corner and identified me with a single gesture. The Marquis took from his pocket the letter I had written, showed it to me, and burnt it while I watched. Then I was brought here, to this cell in the Bastille.

"The two brothers, of the St. Evrémonde family, have destroyed me and my family. To them and their descendants, to the last of their race, I, Alexandre Manette, unhappy prisoner, do this last night of the year 1767, in my unbearable agony, denounce them to heaven and to earth."

A terrible sound arose when the reading of this document was done. The audience, who had been silent during the account, burst forth in a frenzy of pent-up excitement and anger. Even when the President called for quiet, the crowd could not, would not, be still.

"Much influence around him, has that Doctor?" murmured Madame Defarge, smiling to The Vengeance. "Save him now, my Doctor, save him!"

At every juryman's vote, there was a roar. Another and another. Roar and roar.

Unanimously voted. Charles Evrémonde, known as Darnay, at heart and by descent an aristocrat, an enemy of the Republic, a notorious oppressor of the People, would return to the prison and be put to death within four-and-twenty hours!

BOOK THREE

Dusk

When the verdict was read, Lucie fell to her knees as if she had been mortally wounded. But, just as quickly, she pulled herself back up again and turned her eyes to search out the eyes of the condemned man.[1]

She stood stretching out her arms towards her husband with nothing in her face but love and consolation. "If I might touch him! If I might embrace him once! O, good citizens, if you just allow it!"

There was but a gaoler left, along with two of the four men who had taken him last night, and

---

[1] Now, Dickens starts to show how strong, calm, and rational Lucie really is. Lucie's role in the book is to provide a moral center from which other people get strength.

Barsad. The people had all poured out to the show in the streets. Barsad proposed to the rest, "Let her embrace him then; it is but a moment." The other guards silently agreed, and passed her over the seats in the hall to a raised place, where he, by leaning over the dock, could fold her in his arms.

"Farewell, dear darling of my soul. We shall meet again where the weary are at rest!" These were her husband's words as he held her tightly.

"I can bear it, dear Charles. I am supported from above: don't suffer for me. A parting blessing for our child."

"I send it to her by you. I kiss her by you. I say farewell to her by you."

"My husband. No! A moment!" He was tearing himself apart from her. "We shall not be separated long. I feel that this will break my heart by-and-by; but I will do my duty while I can, and when I leave her, God will raise up friends for her, as He did for me."

Doctor Manette had followed Lucie, and would have fallen on his knees to both of them, except Darnay put out a hand and seized him, crying: "No, no! What have you done that you should kneel to me! I know now what you suffered in prison! I thank you with all my heart, and all my love and duty. Heaven be with you, dear sir!"

As he was drawn away, his wife released him, and stood looking after him with her hands touching one another in the attitude of prayer, and with a radiant look upon her face, in which there was even a comforting smile. As he went out the prisoners' door, she turned, laid her head on her father's breast, tried to speak to him, and then fell at his feet.

Then, moving from the dark corner from which he had never moved, Sydney Carton came and lifted her off the ground. His arms trembled as they raised her, and supported her head. Yet, there was an air about him that wasn't all of pity—that had a flush of pride in it.

He carried her lightly to the door and laid her tenderly on the seat of her coach. Her father and Mr. Lorry got into it, and Carton took a seat beside the driver.

When they arrived at the gateway, Carton lifted her again, and carried her up the stairs to their rooms. There, he laid her down on a couch where her child and Miss Pross wept over her.

"Oh, Carton, Carton, dear Carton!" cried little Lucie, springing up and throwing her arms round him in a burst of grief. "Now that you have come, I think you will do something to help Mamma, something to save Papa! O, look at her, dear Carton! Can you, of all the people who love her, bear to see her so?"

He bent over the child, and laid her blooming cheek against his face. Then he put her gently from him and looked at her unconscious mother.

"Before I go," he said to her father, "I may kiss her?"

When he bent down and touched her face with his lips, he murmured some words. The child, who was nearest to him, told them afterwards, and told her grandchildren, when she was a handsome old lady, that she heard him say, "A life you love."[2]

Sydney Carton left Lucie and made his way into the outer room. He looked over at Mr. Lorry and saw the man's grief. "I have no hope," said Mr. Lorry, in a sorrowful whisper.

"Nor have I. I heard the fall of the guillotine in the sound of the crowd in court. He will die: there is no real hope," said Carton. "Listen carefully, my dear friend. You must attend to what I say and ask no questions. Can you do it for her and for the little child?"

---

[2] A life you love—remember Book Two, when Carton told Lucie, "I will help you, or a life you love."

"Of course."

"Here is the certificate that allows me to pass out of the city. Look at it. You see—Sydney Carton, an Englishman?"

Mr. Lorry held it open in his hand, gazing into Carton's earnest face.

"Keep it for me until tomorrow. I shall see Darnay tomorrow, you remember; and I had better not take it into the prison.

"Also, take this paper that Dr. Manette has carried about him. It is a similar certificate, letting him and his daughter and her child at any time pass the barrier and return to England. You see?"

"Yes!"

"This paper is good, until recalled. But it may be soon recalled, and, I have reason to think, will be."

"They are not in danger?"

"They are in great danger. They are in danger of **denunciation**[3] by Madame Defarge. Lucie and little Lucie—they too have the Evrémonde name. But don't look so horrified. You will save them all."

"Heaven grant I may, Carton! But how?"

"I'll tell you how. This new denunciation will certainly not take place until after tomorrow. You

---

[3] **denunciation**—accusation.

know it is a capital crime to mourn for a victim of the guillotine. She and her father will unquestionably be guilty of this crime. Madame Defarge will be watching.

"Early tomorrow have a horse and carriage ready for your return trip to England."

"It shall be done!"

"You are a noble heart. Tell her, tonight, that she and her child and father are in danger. Dwell upon that, for she would willingly lay her own fair head beside her husband's. Tell her that for the sake of her child and her father, they must all leave Paris, with you, at two o'clock in the afternoon. Tell her that it was her husband's last wish. Tell her that more depends upon it than she dare believe, or hope.

"The moment I arrive at your carriage tomorrow, take me in and drive away. Stop for nothing."

"I understand that I wait for you under all circumstances?"

"You have my certificate in your hand with the rest, you know, and will reserve my place. Wait for nothing else but to have my place occupied, and then for England! Swear to me that nothing will influence you to change the course on which we now stand pledged to one another."

"Nothing, Carton."

"Remember these words tomorrow: change the course, or delay in it—for any reason—and no life can possibly be saved, and many lives will be sacrificed."

Swear to me that nothing will influence you to change the course on which we now stand pledged to one another.

"I will remember my vow. I hope to do my part faithfully."

"And I hope to do mine. Now, good-bye!"

Carton walked out into the dark night. He entered the courtyard and remained there for a few moments alone, looking up at the light in the window of Lucie's room. Before he went away, he breathed a blessing towards it, and said farewell.

Sydney Carton paused in the street, not quite decided where to go. After walking awhile he finally resolved, "It is best that these people should know there is such a man as I here." As he went toward Saint Antoine, he stopped at a shop window and slightly altered his coat collar and his wild hair. This done, he went direct to Defarge's.

Carton asked for a small measure of wine in very poor French. "English?" asked Madame Defarge.

"Yes, madame, I am English."

As Madame Defarge returned to her counter to get the wine, he heard her say, "I swear to you, he looks just like Evrémonde!"

Carton read a newspaper, following the lines and words with a slow forefinger, and with a studious and absorbed face. Defarge and Madame Defarge, after a short silence, resumed their conversation with The Vengeance.

"As to you," said Madame, addressing her husband, "if it depended on you—which, happily, it does not—you would rescue this man even now."

"No!" protested Defarge, "I would not! But I would leave the matter there. I say, stop there."

"My husband, I was brought up among the fishermen of the seashore, and that peasant family so injured by the two Evrémonde brothers, as that Bastille paper describes, is my family. Defarge, that sister of the mortally wounded boy was my sister, that husband was my sister's husband, that unborn child was their child, that brother was my brother, that father was my father, those dead are my dead, and that summons to answer for those things descends to me! Do you understand?"[4]

Defarge nodded.

"Then tell wind and fire where to stop," returned Madame; "but don't tell me."

Customers entered, and the group was broken up. The English customer paid for his wine, counted his change with difficulty, and left the shop.

---

[4] This speech from Madame Defarge explains why she feels so much bitterness toward Darnay, Lucie, and little Lucie. She despises anyone associated with the Evrémonde name.

Fifty-two

In the black prison, the doomed of the day awaited their fate. Fifty-two were to go that afternoon to the guillotine.

Charles Darnay, alone in a cell, sustained himself with prayer. He knew that no personal influence could save him and that he was to die in just a few hours.

Nevertheless, it was not easy, with the face of his beloved wife fresh before him, to compose his mind to what it must bear. He wrote a long letter to Lucie, showing her that he had known nothing of her father's imprisonment until he had heard of it from herself, and that he had been as ignorant as she of his father's and uncle's responsibility for that misery.

To Dr. Manette, he wrote in the same strain; but he told her father that he was giving his wife and child to his care. He told him this, very strongly, with the hope of rousing him from any despondency or depression.

To Mr. Lorry, he entrusted them all, and explained his worldly affairs. When that was done, all was done. He never thought of Carton. His mind was so full of the others that he never once thought of him.

He had never seen the instrument that was to end his life. How high it was from the ground, how many steps it had, where he would stand, how he would be touched, which way his face would be turned, whether he would be the first, or might be the last. These and many similar questions flashed through his mind over and over again. Never were they connected with fear; he was conscious of no fear. Rather, he wanted to know what to do when the time came.

Never were they connected with fear; he was conscious of no fear.

He had been told that the final hour was three o'clock, but he knew he would be summoned earlier because the **tumbrels**[1] moved so heavily and slowly through the streets.

At one o'clock, he heard footsteps in the stone passage outside the door. He braced himself and continued praying.

The key was put in the lock and turned. The door was quickly opened and closed, and there stood before him, face to face, quiet, intent upon him, with the light of a smile on his features, and a cautionary finger on his lip, Sydney Carton.

"Of all the people upon earth, you least expected to see me?" Carton asked.

"I cannot believe it is you! You are not a prisoner?" he asked.

"No. I have a power over one of the turnkeys here. I come from her—your wife, dear Darnay. I bring you a request from her."

"What is it?"

"A most earnest plea. There is no time to ask me why I bring it, or what it means; I have no time to tell you. You must comply with it—take off those boots you wear, and put on these of mine."

There was a chair against the wall of the cell, behind the prisoner. Carton, pressing forward, had

---

[1] **tumbrels**—open carts in which people were driven to their execution during the French Revolution.

already got him down into it and stood over him, barefoot.

"Put on these boots of mine. Quick!"

"Carton, there is no escaping from this place; it never can be done. You will only die with me. It is madness."

"It would be madness if I asked you to escape; but have I? Change that tie for this of mine and that coat for this of mine. While you do it, let me take this ribbon from your hair, and shake out your hair like this of mine!"

With a wonderful quickness, Carton forced all these changes upon him. The prisoner was like a young child in his hands.

"Carton! Dear Carton! It is madness. It can never be done. It has been attempted, and has always failed. I implore you not to add your death to the bitterness of mine."

"Do I ask you, my dear Darnay, to go through the door? When I ask that, refuse. There are pen and ink and paper on this table. Is your hand steady enough to write?"

"It was when you came in."

"Steady it again, and write what I dictate. Quick, friend, quick! Write exactly as I speak."

"If you remember," said Carton, dictating, "the words that passed between us long ago, you will understand this when you see it. You do remember them, I know. It is not in your nature to forget them."

As Carton spoke, he drew his hand from his breast pocket; by chance, the prisoner looked up.

"Is that a weapon in your hand?"

"No; I am not armed."

"What is it in your hand?"

"You shall know soon. Write on; there are but a few words more." He dictated again. "I am thankful that the time has come when I can prove them. That I do so is no subject for regret or grief." As he said these words with his eyes fixed on the writer, his hand slowly and softly moved down close to the writer's face.

The pen dropped from Darnay's fingers on the table, and he looked about him vacantly. "What **vapor**[2] is that?" he asked.

"Vapor? I smell nothing; there is nothing here. Take up the pen and finish. Hurry!"

Again the hand was at the prisoner's face. The prisoner sprang up with a **reproachful**[3] look, but Carton's hand was close and firm at his nostrils, and Carton's left arm caught him round the waist.

---

[2] **vapor**—mist, fumes, or smoke.

[3] **reproachful**—blaming.

For a few seconds Darnay struggled with the man who had come to lay down his life for him; but, within a minute or so, he was stretched **insensible**[4] on the ground.

Quickly, but with hands as true to the purpose as his heart was, Carton dressed himself in the clothes the prisoner had laid aside, combed back his hair, and tied it with the ribbon the prisoner had worn. Then, he softly called, "Enter there! Come in!" and Barsad presented himself.

"You see?" said Carton, looking up, as he kneeled on one knee beside the insensible figure, putting the paper in the breast pocket: "Is your danger very great?"

"Mr. Carton," the spy answered, with a timid snap of his fingers, "my danger is small if you are true to the whole of your bargain."

"Don't fear me. I will be true to the death."

"You must be, Mr. Carton, if the tale of fifty-two[5] is to be right."

"Have no fear! I shall soon be out of the way of harming you, and the rest will soon be far from here, please God! Now, get assistance and take me to the coach."

---

[4] **insensible**—unconscious.

[5] fifty-two—the number of prisoners scheduled for the guillotine that day.

"You?"

"Him, man, with whom I have exchanged. Tell them this: I was weak and faint when you brought me in, and I am fainter now as you take me out. The parting interview has overpowered me. Such a thing has happened here, often. Your life is in your own hands. Quick! Call assistance!"

The spy withdrew, and Carton seated himself at the table, resting his forehead on his hands. The spy returned immediately with two men.

"How, then?" said one of them, looking at the fallen figure. "He fainted at the thought that his friend has won the prize of the guillotine?"

They raised the unconscious figure, placed it on a **litter**[6] they had brought to the door, and bent to carry it away.

"The time is short, Evrémonde," said the spy, in a warning voice.

"I know it well," answered Carton. "Be careful of my friend, I beg you, and leave me."

"Come, then, lift him out of here," said Barsad.

The door closed, and Carton was left alone. He listened quietly for an alarm, but there was none. No cry was raised or hurry made that seemed unusual. Breathing more freely, he sat down at the

---

[6] **litter**—a framework or cot in which the wounded or ill are transported.

table, and listened again until the clock struck two.

Sounds that he was not afraid of, for he knew their meaning, then began to be audible. Several doors were opened in succession, and finally his own. A gaoler, with a list in his hand, looked in, merely saying, "Follow me, Evrémonde!" He followed the guard into a large dark room.

A very few moments after he arrived, a young woman, with a pale, thin, sweet face, rose from the seat where he had observed her sitting, and came to speak to him.

"Citizen Evrémonde," she said, touching him with her cold hand. "I am a poor little seamstress, who was with you in La Force."

He replied: "True. I forget what you were accused of?"

"Plots. Though heaven knows that I am innocent of any. Is it likely? Who would think of plotting with a poor little weak creature like me?" The forlorn smile with which she said it, so touched him that tears started from his eyes.

"I am not afraid to die, Citizen Evrémonde, but I have done nothing. If I may ride with you, Citizen Evrémonde, will you let me hold your hand? I am not afraid, but I am little and weak, and it will give me more courage."

As the patient eyes were lifted to his face, he saw a sudden doubt in them, and then astonishment. He pressed the work-worn young fingers, and touched his lips to hush her.

"Are you dying for him?" she whispered.

"And his wife and child. Hush! Yes."

"O, you will let me hold your brave hand, stranger?"

"Hush! Yes, my poor sister, to the last."

The same shadows that are falling on the prison are falling, in that same hour of the early afternoon, on the barrier with the crowd about it when a coach going out of Paris drives up to be examined.

"Who goes here? Whom have we within? Papers!"

The papers are handed out, and read.

"Alexandre Manette. Physician. French. Lucie Manette, his daughter, French. Lucie, her child, English. Mr. Sydney Carton. English. Apparently the Englishman is in a swoon?"

"It is hoped he will recover in the fresher air."

"Jarvis Lorry. Banker. English. Which is he?"

"I am he."

"Behold your papers, Jarvis Lorry, counter-signed."

"One can depart, citizen?"

"One can depart. Forward, my postilions! A good journey!"

There is terror in the carriage, there is weeping, there is the heavy breathing of the insensible traveler.

"Are we not going too slowly? Can they not be made to go faster?" asks Lucie, clinging to the old man.

"It would seem like flight, my darling. I must not urge them too much; it would rouse suspicion."

"Look back, look back, and see if we are pursued!"

"The road is clear, my dearest. So far, we are not pursued."

The night comes on dark. He moves more; he is beginning to revive and to speak; he thinks they are still together; he asks him, by his name, what he has in his hand.

O pity us! Heaven help us! Look out, look out, and see if we are pursued. The wind is rushing after us, and the clouds are flying after us, and the moon is plunging after us, and the whole wild night is in pursuit of us; but so far, we are pursued by nothing else.

BOOK THREE

The Knitting Done

At that same time when the fifty-two awaited their fate, Madame Defarge held a dark council with The Vengeance and Jacques Three.

"The time to act is now," began Madame. "The Evrémonde people are to be exterminated. The wife and child must follow the husband and father."

"She has a fine head for it," croaked Jacques Three with enjoyment. "The child also. And we seldom have a child there. It is a pretty sight!"

"We will move today," said Madame. "She will be at home awaiting the moment of his death. She will be grieving. She will be in a state of mind that interferes with the justice of the Republic. She will

230   **A Tale of Two Cities**

be full of sympathy with its enemies. I will go to her."

"Take you my knitting," said Madame Defarge, placing it in the hands of The Vengeance, "and have it ready for me in my usual seat near the guillotine."

"I willingly obey the orders of my chief," said The Vengeance, kissing her cheek. "You will not be late?"

"I shall be there before the tumbrels arrive," said Madame.

The meeting thus ended, Madame started off in the direction of Lucie's rooms. Walking with confidence and pride, she took her way along the streets.

At the same time that Madame was hosting her small meeting, Miss Pross and Jerry Cruncher were preparing to leave the city. "I am so distracted with fear for our precious creatures," said Miss Pross, wildly crying, "that I cannot think clearly!"

"Let us hurry, so that we can meet up with their coach at the Channel crossing," reminded Jerry.

And still Madame Defarge came nearer and nearer.

"As planned, I will meet you at three o'clock in the courtyard, so that we may board our coach. Now hurry, Jerry, and don't be a moment late!"

Without a word, Jerry rushed out the front door, leaving Miss Pross to finish the packing.

Still Madame Defarge came nearer and nearer.

She looked at her watch, and it was twenty minutes past two. She had no time to lose. But first she got a basin of water to wash her red eyes, constantly pausing and looking around. In one of those pauses, she jumped back and cried out, for someone was standing in the room. Madame Defarge looked coldly at her, and said, "The wife of Evrémonde; where is she?"

"You might, from your appearance, be the wife of the devil," said Miss Pross. "Nevertheless, you shall not get the better of me. I am an Englishwoman."

Madame Defarge looked at her scornfully. "It will do her no good to keep herself hidden," said Madame Defarge. "Go tell her that I wish to see her. Do you hear?"

Each woman spoke in her own language, neither understood the other's words, but both were very watchful.

"No, you wicked foreign woman! I am your match."

"You imbecile!" said Madame Defarge, frowning. "I demand to see her." With an angry cry, Madame Defarge made a quick search of the apartment. "I will tear you to pieces, if I must. Tell me where she and the child are hidden!" said Madame Defarge.

"Tell me where she and the child are hidden!" said Madame Defarge.

Madame lunged at Miss Pross, who grabbed her around the waist and held her tight. Madame Defarge punched and tore at her face; but Miss Pross, with her head down, held her round the waist, and refused to budge an inch. She fought with the vigor of love, always so much stronger than hate.

Soon, Madame Defarge's hands ceased to strike and felt at her encircled waist.

"Your knife is under my arm," said Miss Pross, in smothered tones. "You shall not draw it! I am stronger than you, and I bless heaven for it. I'll hold you till one or other of us faints or dies!"

Madame Defarge's hands were at her bosom. Miss Pross looked up, saw that she held a gun, struck out at it, and, suddenly, stood alone—blinded with smoke.

All this was in a second. As the smoke cleared, leaving an awful stillness, it passed out on the air like the soul of the furious woman whose body lay lifeless on the ground. Miss Pross stared at the body of her enemy for a moment more, and then just as quickly gathered her things and ran from the rooms. It was time to meet the coach that would take her home.

BOOK THREE

The Footsteps Die Out Forever

Along the Paris streets, the death carts rumble,
hollow and harsh. Six tumbrels carry the day's
prisoners to La Guillotine.

As the **somber**[1] wheels of the six carts go round,
they seem to plow up a long, crooked path among
the people in the streets. People call out to the tumbrels, screaming curses, urging the drivers to hurry,
hurry to the guillotine.

Some of the riders in the tumbrels stare out at
the people. Others close their eyes and think, or try
to get their thoughts together. Only one, and he a

---

[1] **somber**—dark.

miserable creature, is so shattered and made drunk by horror that he sings and tries to dance. Beside the third tumbrel rides John Barsad, the spy.

"Which is Evrémonde?" comes the call.

"There he is. At the back there, with his hand in the girl's."

The man cries, "Down, Evrémonde. To the guillotine all aristocrats! Down, Evrémonde!"

"Hush, hush!" the spy entreats him, timidly. "Let him be at peace."

But the crowd continues to call out, "Down, Evrémonde!"

> **"Down, Evrémonde. To the guillotine all aristocrats! Down, Evrémonde!"**

The clocks are on the stroke of three. The tumbrels have arrived. Standing on a chair is The Vengeance. "Thérèse!" she cries, in her shrill tones. "Who has seen her? Thérèse Defarge!"

"She has never missed before," says a knitting-woman of the sisterhood.

"Bad fortune!" cries The Vengeance, stamping her foot, "and here are the tumbrels! Evrémonde will be killed in a wink, and she not here! See her knitting in my hand, and her empty chair ready for her. I cry with **vexation**[2] and disappointment!"

---

[2] **vexation**—irritation.

The tumbrels begin to discharge their loads. The ministers of the guillotine are robed and ready. Crash!—A head is held up, and the knitting-women who scarcely lifted their eyes to look at it a moment ago when it could think and speak, count One.

The second tumbrel empties and moves on; the third comes up. Crash—And the knitting-women, never faltering or pausing in their work, count Two.

The supposed Evrémonde descends, and the seamstress is lifted out after him. He has not let her patient hand go in getting out, but still holds it as he promised. He gently places her with her back to the crashing engine that constantly whirrs up and falls, and she looks into his face and thanks him.

"If it weren't for you, dear stranger, I should not be so brave," she whispered.

"You have done the same for me," says Sydney Carton. "Keep your eyes upon me, dear child, and mind no other object."

"I mind nothing while I hold your hand. I shall mind nothing when I let it go, if they are rapid."

"They will be rapid. Fear not!"

The two stand in the fast-thinning throng of victims, but they speak as if they were alone. Eye to eye, voice to voice, hand to hand, heart to heart, these two stand.

"You comfort me so much!" she whispers to Carton." I am so ignorant. Am I to kiss you now? Is the moment come?"

"Yes."

She kisses his lips; he kisses hers; they solemnly bless each other. The spare hand does not tremble as he releases it; nothing worse than a sweet, bright constancy is in the patient face. She goes next before him—is gone; the knitting-women count Twenty-two.

"I am the Resurrection and the Life, saith the Lord: he that believeth in me, though he were dead, yet shall he live: and whosoever liveth and believeth in me shall never die."

The murmuring of many voices, the upturning of many faces, the pressing on of many footsteps in the outskirts of the crowd, so that it swells forward in a mass, like one great heave of water, all flashes away. Twenty-three.

They said of him, about the city that night, that it was the most peaceful face ever to look out at the crowd. Many added that he looked **sublime**.[3]

---

[3] **sublime**—awe-inspiring.

O
ne of the most remarkable sufferers by the same ax—a woman—had asked at the foot of the same scaffold, not long before, to be allowed to write down the thoughts that were inspiring her. If Carton had been able to write his, and if they were prophetic, they would have been these:

"I see Barsad, and Cly, Defarge, The Vengeance, the Juryman, the Judge, and the new oppressors, who have risen on the destruction of the old, dying by this same instrument. I see a beautiful city and a brilliant people who have struggled to be free. I see the evil of this time and of the previous time wearing itself out, for evil cannot last forever.

"I see the lives, for which I lay down my life, peaceful, useful, prosperous and happy in that England that I shall see no more. I see Lucie with a child named for me. I see her father, aged and bent, but otherwise restored, and faithful to all men in his healing office, and at peace. I see the good old man, so long their friend, in ten years' time passing tranquilly to his reward.

"I see that I hold a place in their hearts, and in the hearts of their children's children, generations hence. I see her, an old woman, weeping for me on the anniversary of this day.

"I see that child, who lay upon her bosom and who has my name, as a man winning his way up in that path of life that once was mine. I see him winning it so well that my name is made **illustrious**[4] by the light of his. I see him bringing a boy of my name, with a forehead that I know and golden hair, to this place. I hear him tell the child my story, with a tender and a faltering voice.

"It is a far, far better thing that I do, than I have ever done; it is a far, far better rest that I go to than I have ever known."[5]

THE END

---

[4] **illustrious**—well known and very distinguished; eminent.

[5] This last sentence is as well known as the first sentence of the book.